every
SHADE
of
HUMAN

this isn't poetry.
it's emotional damage with line breaks.
nothing scripted. nothing softened.
just human.
unedited feelings, rebranded as literature.

Serenite Hope

ISBN: 979-8-9993596-1-2
Cover design and interior layout by Serenite Hope

Hey you,
Yes—you, holding this book in your hands.
I don't know how you found your way here,
but I'm glad you did.

This isn't a traditional collection.
There's no table of contents. No chapters.
Most pieces don't even have titles.
They're not missing—they're unlabeled on purpose.
Because thoughts don't announce themselves before arriving.
Because healing doesn't happen in neat little sections.
Because being human has never been linear.

This book is meant to move like a mind—shifting tones, turning corners, looping back on itself, interrupting something soft with something sharp. Some pieces may speak loudly to you. Others may whisper past. That's okay. Every shade doesn't have to match your skin to reflect your story.

You might cry on a page you weren't expecting. You might laugh mid-sentence. You might just stare at a line thinking, who let her say that out loud? That's kind of the point. This is a place for everything—the sacred, the silly, the unspeakable, the true.

I'm not trying to impress you.
I'm just trying to be honest.

Read this book in order,
or don't.
Sit with it all at once,
or come back to it like an old friend.
Whatever you choose,
I hope you feel seen in some small way.
Or at the very least,
feel a little less alone.

Welcome inside my head.
It's messy here, but it's real.
Take what you need.
Leave the rest.

Serenite

the door creaks open
not to let you understand—
but to let you feel.
some truths don't need translation
to be heard by the body.

when they all gather,
no one wants to take the lead—
but still, we begin.

Logic checked in with a clipboard and pen,
Demanded receipts and a flowchart again.
Emotion arrived in a whirlwind of cries,
With glitter and trauma and twenty red flags.

"This isn't efficient," Logic declared,
As Emotion sat sobbing and wildly impaired.
"I made tea for my feelings," she said with a pout,
"Then drank it too fast and now I'm burnt out."

– – –

Logic tried listing the pros and the cons.
Emotion just wailed, "But the vibe was all wrong!"
They both tried to sit on the very same chair,
Then argued for hours over who put it there.

Emotion wrote poems at 3AM sharp.
Logic revised them into legal remarks.
One wanted closure, the other wanted proof.
They both got evicted from their own damn truth.

In the mirror they saw someone crooked
but whole—
And both blamed each other for losing control.
But neither would leave, and neither would bend,

So they learned to co-sign the chaos...
as friends.

—

Enter Body — uninvited, barefoot, bold,
Wearing yesterday's hoodie and three-day-old cold.
"Sup," she says, cracking every joint with flair,
Then dumps her entire trauma on the only clean
chair.

"We weren't ready for guests," Logic began.
"We are the guest!" Body yelled, rubbing her hand.
"You don't even feel this," Emotion snapped loud.
"I am the feeling!" Body gasped, very proud.

Now it's a circus of joints and thoughts:
One counts calories, the other gets lost.
Emotion wants yoga with candles and cries.
Logic says, "Please hydrate or one of us dies."

"I'm stiff where I used to be fluid and strong."
"I warned you," said Logic. *"You sat wrong too long."*
"I feel ugly today," Emotion chimed in.
Body just shrugged, *"Then dance like a sin."*

They argue in mirrors.
They wrestle in sleep.
They compromise only
on carbs and grief.

Some days, they rally. Some days, they break.
Some days, Body just wants another **damn cake.**
But they're learning, these three —
the hard, human way —
To listen, to rest, and let all of them stay.

—

They didn't notice at first —
Soul doesn't knock.
She just arrives.
Like wind through a cracked window,
or a truth you forgot you knew.

She sat on the floor, legs crossed like roots,
Said nothing, just breathed —
long enough to make Logic squirm.

"Is she... buffering?" Logic whispered.

Emotion paused mid-rant, mascara on chin.
Body stopped stretching and scratched at her skin.
The room went still, the way dusk holds its breath.

Then Soul finally spoke:

"Y'all are loud. But I love you."

Body blinked. Emotion cried (obviously).
Logic tried to take notes but the pen ran dry.
Soul kept going, in that too-soft voice
that somehow made everyone feel seen and scolded:

"You think you're broken, but you're just... layered."
"You think you're late, but you're right on time."
"You think your worth is in motion or feeling or proof—
but it's in the watching. In the stillness.
In the you beneath you."

They all sat with that.
Even Logic didn't rebut.
Even Emotion didn't cry (for like... ten whole
seconds).
Even Body stopped fidgeting.

Because when Soul shows up,
nobody's the boss —
and yet everything feels held.

And for once,
they didn't try to fix or feel or flee.
They just **stayed**—
with the **mess,**
with the **love,**
with the whole
of **being.**

I wish I could say
"Today I see her."
That girl I bloomed into at twelve.
That face that finally met the world
and was met, in return.

But it seems every decade of life
signs a secret pact
to plot against our clarity.
Each one handing you
some new reason to squint
at your own reflection.

My newest?
A shift in symmetry.
A tilt to this body
that no longer looks like the one I worked so hard to
grow into.

So when men
even politely
call me *"pretty lady,"*
I raise my inner eyebrow
and think:

"Sir, are your standards low,

or are we both fives
hovering in mutual delusion?"

It's not bitterness.
It's... *math.*
It's *mirror fatigue.*
It's the exhausting kindness of strangers
sounding like mockery
because you've unlearned
how to believe praise.

But maybe—
just maybe—
the body doesn't need to be beautiful
to be a whole self.

And maybe suspicion
isn't the enemy of confidence—
maybe it's just the armor we wear
until *acceptance feels safe.*

—

You don't have to say "I see her."
You're allowed to say:
"I don't quite see her,
but I remember her.
I walk beside her.
And I'm still trying to believe what others say
without laughing first."

In each quiet gesture,
when a man speaks with his hands—
I drop things on purpose.

It wasn't the words—
he didn't use them.
He texted, tapped, typed.
But I understood him
long before the screen lit up.

It was in his hands.

Not rough,
but not soft either.
Masculine in the quietest way—
a shape sculpted by usefulness,
not vanity.
Veins tracing certainty.
Fingers the perfect width—
not too long,
not too short,
nail beds clean, unspoken.
Not a model's polish,
not a laborer's callous—
just... capable.

His hands looked like
they'd hold a hot bowl without flinching,
tie a child's shoelace,

press a message into your back
without needing words.

No flourish.
No flex.
Just function
and a kind of knowing.

When he moved,
the world moved around him.
When he reached,
you believed he'd never drop what mattered.

And suddenly,
I was **gone.**
Swooning over ten fingers
that never said a single thing aloud—
but somehow
spoke to everything inside me.

I see them before they move.
I feel them before they speak.
And I decide, *without guilt*, to look away.

It's not me being rude.
It's me recognizing **desperation**—
that silent scream in their energy.
The need to be *seen*, *spoken* to, *absorbed*.
They may not say a word,
but the **hunger** is loud—
a gravitational pull dressed up as politeness.

And I've learned,
just because someone wants to talk to me
doesn't mean I'm required to **open the door.**

Not all contact is **connection.**
Not all attention is **mutual.**
Some people approach with **open eyes**
and **closed intentions**—
hoping to plug in,
not exchange.

So I don't make eye contact.
Not to be *cruel*, but to stay **clear**.
Because once we lock eyes,
it becomes an **invitation**.
And not everyone deserves one.

I reserve my **presence**
for the ones who live in the moment,
not those projecting their emptiness into mine.

That's not me being **cold**.
That's me being **well**.

Eyes narrowed, I watch.
This is not a crush.
Just conducting quiet research.

Lately, I've caught myself giving people the side eye.
Not just any side eye—
the squinty, suspicious,
trying-to-read-your-aura side eye.
And mostly men.
Specifically: grown, unattached,
no-visible-ring men.
Not because I want to know them.
Because I want to know—
who are you sleeping with?

Like truly.
Where are you...
putting that energy?
Who's letting you in?
Are you rotating through a collection?
Revisiting your ex?
Destroying someone's self-esteem in secret?
Or just out here in these streets,
raw and emotionally unavailable?

I'm not judging.
Okay—*I am*, a little.
But mostly I'm bewildered.
Like watching a squirrel try to drive a car.

Just pure chaos behind the eyes.

Because people love to say
"I'm single"
but forget to add
"...but not celibate."

And listen—
I know grown folks can do what they want.
But the older I get,
the more I feel like unclaimed intimacy
is just **clutter.**
Spiritual clutter.
Emotional landmines waiting to explode
in the next situationship
you pretend isn't a situationship.

So yeah.
If you see me watching you from across the room
with a look that says
*"I have questions but no energy to ask
them"*—
you're probably right.

I just wanna know:
who are you sleeping with?
Because that will tell me everything
you're not saying out loud.

I cried over a boy once.
Just the once.

Not because I hurt him—
because I didn't—
but because I *betrayed myself.*

I made a promise,
and my word has always been
my bond,
even in suffering.

So to realize I wanted—
no, *needed*—
something more
felt like *treason.*
Against my own soul.

And I cried.
Not the polite pageant cry
with a finger to catch
a socially acceptable tear.

I cried ugly.
Possessed ugly.
Sounding like
Klingon Chewbacca
mid-exorcism.

And in that torrent,
I hadn't yet realized
the path I'd chosen
was *hell*
dressed in the *cut-and-paste glow*
of my vision board.

But I felt better
after that cry.

I think I buried someone that day.

Not My Song.

*I was eight—the flower girl in a red dress for my
mother's wedding.*
She was finally getting married, after three
daughters with three different men.
Unfortunately, it was to a man who fathered none of
us.

A man I always knew was a perverted creep—
but I digress.

We rehearsed how I'd walk down the aisle
once the piano lady played a specific song.
I was to step forward slowly, dropping petals—
right, left, right, left—on either side.
As long as she kept playing, I'd keep walking.
With my logic-brained personality,
they really should have seen this coming.

The day of the wedding,
I made it halfway down the aisle
before some demon took over the piano lady.
She switched the song
like a DJ on Ladies' Night.

I froze mid-step, mid-petal-throw—

eyes bulging with the sheer audacity.
The instructions were clear.
This was not the song.

Guests whispered.
Hands reached out, trying to coax or drag me.
I stood rooted, dodging their attempts,
my wide-eyed face a silent protest.
I kept staring between the guests and the piano lady
like:

Y'all hear this too, right?

Eventually—mercifully—she switched back.
I smiled, picked up where I left off,
but not before tossing a dramatic eye-roll
that could've shaken the chapel walls.

Someone caught the whole thing on tape.
Growing up, we'd rewatch it now and then,
laughing until tears rolled.
I guess even back then,
I knew not to walk blindly
when the music didn't feel right.

Not My Crowd.

The reception was chaos.
I walked into the hall and nearly froze.
People were acting like they hadn't seen food
in three lifetimes—
and were fully convinced
they never would again.

There were multiple cakes for the guests,
not just the bridal cake,
but that didn't matter.
They were shoving, slicing,
grabbing chunks of cake
like it was falling from heaven and melting on impact.

What ruffled my feathers most?
They cut the wedding cake.
The wedding cake.
And left only the tiniest top tier—
the one with the little bride and groom on it—
for us, the actual bridal family,
to take home.
How generous.

But I digress.

Once the cake frenzy died down
and people were eating real food like humans again,
the music started.
People danced.
Children danced.
And I... did not.

From what I could tell,
the adults were dancing together
and the children were doing something that vaguely
resembled movement
but mostly looked like *sugar-fueled chaos.*
I had no intention of joining them.
I didn't know what they were doing
and frankly, **I didn't want to know.**

So I sat in my chair,
wiggling to the rhythm,
content to groove in my own private circle
of superiority and bass.

Someone caught that on tape too—
me in my red dress,
shoulders bouncing,
bobbing side to side *like I had a secret.*

Eventually, someone said,
"Why don't you go dance?"

And everyone laughed.

So I did.

I marched right over to the adult circle
and danced my little booty off
in the middle of them all—
center of attention,
no invitation needed.

The grown-ups gasped, cheered, pointed,
laughed in delight.
Meanwhile, *I ignored the kids completely.*
That was not my crowd.

Even then,
I knew where I belonged.
And it wasn't with the ones
still figuring out the rhythm.

They extend their hands
but I have already seen
what moves underneath.

She flagged me down like she just couldn't bear to
let the moment pass.
"I've seen you a few times," she said, reaching
toward me with the gentlest smile and the most
dangerous hand.

Her palm was open. But her spirit wasn't.

Still, I smiled. My peace was intact.
I had slept well the night before.
I was glowing from the inside out.
There was a lightness in my voice, and clarity in my
bones.
I was in that high-frequency softness that makes
people mistake you for someone open to *everything*.

So I replied kindly—genuinely: "Oh, I don't shake
hands, but I'll give you a fist bump."

It was respectful. Honest. A boundary delivered on a
silk pillow.

She clutched her pearls.
Folded her mouth.
Adjusted her cardigan.

And before I could even offer her my name, she
turned and walked away.

I raised my voice to call it after her, just so it
wouldn't hang unfinished in the air.
And then I let her go.

Because I know that look.
That subtle flicker of disappointment when someone
realizes their little reach couldn't reach *me*.

She wanted to touch my hand and take something.
Just a little. Just enough to feed the part of her that
felt dull and drained. She didn't want to know me.
She wanted to **access** me.

But I've learned—
when your energy is clean, calm, and full of breath,
people will try to drink from you without asking.

They'll mistake your glow for permission.
They'll touch you with hands that look innocent
but carry a thousand invisible needs.

I don't shake hands anymore.
I offer the **Fist of Peace**—
not because they've earned it,
but because it's the loudest "No" I can give
while still smiling.

Bone on Bone

I asked you to hold my hand,
to stand beside me
the way we did on the day we made our vows.
You didn't say no.
But your silence—
it screamed.
Louder than any word you've ever said.

It crept under my skin,
burrowed through flesh,
settled in my bones.

Now it vibrates.
It rattles every time I remind you of the promises
you made,
and you call it *nagging.*

Bone on bone.
When the cries of your children
don't concern you enough to move.

Bone scraping bone.
When you ignore me—
or worse, *pretend* to listen
as I recount the shape of my day.

Bone stabbing bone.
When someone else's opinion
matters more than mine.
When I hear you repeat my words
three months too late—
now they make sense,
now they matter,
because they *didn't* come from me.

Bone eviscerating bone.
When you call me *lazy*
on days I can't tell
if I still like the color blue—
or if it's just the first thing my hand landed on.
I feel lost in my skin.
You don't even see me searching.

And I don't know where to refill
what has been siphoned from me
over these years.

So no.
I have *nothing* left to give—
Not to you.
Not to this house.
Not to these little people
wearing your face.

I'm not resting.

I'm not drifting.
I'm disappearing.

I am dying.

Not in the way
that makes people come running.
But the kind of death
that looks like dinner made
and dishes done
and the right size batteries
already in the drawer.

Can't you see?
Can't you hear
the sound of *finality*
in my voice
as I tell you
for the tenth
damn time
where to find your socks?

i never met a boy once
and i gave him
everything
i didn't know yet
how to give myself
not because he earned
or deserved it
but because i needed
someone
somewhere
outside of me
to know what love
truly feels like
when it doesn't ask
or beg
just EXISTS

Curious, Not Cruel

There's a lie we've all started telling—
That we don't look.
That we don't notice.
That we're all so evolved now, we barely register
difference.

But I've been on both ends of the stare—
And baby, we see.

We see the ginger hair that glows like fire under
sunlight,
and we want to touch it.
We see the lashes so thick they curl at the tips,
and we want to ask if they're real.
We see the skin so rich it looks like it was carved
from the last dark hour before dawn—
and we want to know if it feels like velvet or rain.

And still, we lie.

We pretend not to notice what stands out.
We call it politeness.
We say it's manners.
But really, it's *fear in a tuxedo*—

the fear of being labeled rude, ignorant, racist,
invasive.
Because somehow, in this glittering age of "woke,"
to see someone
means you must want to *own* them.

If you're curious about someone's features,
you must be *racist.*
If you compliment a cultural detail,
you must be *appropriating.*
If you stare too long,
you must be *judging.*

But here's the truth:
We all stare.

Every last one of us has been that awkward kid
at the buffet of human beauty,
trying to sample flavors
without being seen drooling.

We've all been caught mid-gawk— face frozen
somewhere between admiration and anthropology—
internally whispering
"stop looking, stop looking, they see you."

We're just not honest about it.

I've stared at Asian eyes
like they were etched in clay with a sculptor's knife.
Sharp. Specific. Unrepeatable.

I've paused at dark skin—
not because it was strange,
but because it looked like *art in motion.*
I've wanted to touch freckles like constellations.
Ask someone how their accent formed—
how many countries it took to build that sound.

But I didn't.
Because I didn't want to be misunderstood.
Because I didn't want someone's blog post to be
about me.

So instead, we all play this game.
Of *Not Seeing.*
Of *Not Asking.*
Of *Not Admitting* that human variation
is one of the most fascinating things about existence.

What if we told the truth?
What if curiosity was allowed again?
What if we let admiration breathe

instead of choking it with disclaimers?

What if a little girl said,

"Your hair shines like a penny in the sun
—can I touch it?"
and instead of calling her a future colonizer,
we said, "Sure, baby. Gently."

What if a boy pointed to brown skin
and asked why it looked like that—
and instead of gasping in horror,
we simply said,
"That's how we were born.
It's just melanin.
It doesn't rub off."

What if we stopped confusing *notice* with *neglect*,
and *curiosity* with *cruelty?*

Because some stares are cruel.
But some are sacred.
Some are *wonder made visible.*

– – –

Let people marvel.
Let people ask.

Let us admit that yes—
we're all constantly scolding ourselves
for being fascinated by each other.

Because honestly?

That's not the worst thing we could be.
Unkindness is.
Superiority is.
Entitlement is.

But *curiosity?*

Curiosity is **human.**
Curiosity is **honest.**
Curiosity is the gateway to connection,
if we'd just let it breathe.

So go ahead.
Stare (politely).
Ask (respectfully).
Admire (openly).

I'm not offended that you see me.

I'd be more offended
if you *didn't.*

a second too fast—
my face betrays what I thought
I had unlearned

My eyes reacted before my heart could reason.
A quick flash of
"not my kind of pretty"—
Followed by a full-bodied scolding from the soul:
"Someone loves them too."

Someone has memorized that laugh.
Stands taller when they smile.
Thinks they hung the stars.

Someone sees beauty in that gait,
charm in that grin,
warmth in what I almost dismissed.

And here I am,
undone in an instant—
Guilty for forgetting what love looks like
when it isn't filtered through my preferences.
When it doesn't ask my permission.
When it shows up anyway
and wraps itself around someone
I almost didn't see.

Still unlearning.

Still becoming the kind of person
who sees people first—
before the lens of preference,
before the echo of culture,
before the habit of judgment.

Human.
Humbled.
Again.

Keep the freedoms
and the **privileges**
of *happiness, anger, sadness, and love*
for yourself.

They belong to **you.**
Not your past.
Not your family.
Not the person who left.
Not the one who stayed but made you shrink.

Let your **joy** arrive *uninvited.*
Let your **rage** have its *day.*
Let your **sorrow** come and go
without needing a reason
anyone else can understand.

Feel what you feel,
because *you feel it—*
not because someone else's choices
deserve your collapse.

No one else should decide
what happens within you
but you.

words fall out too fast
lips obey where soul does not—
"thank you" on repeat

They say "thank you" is free.
But I've learned there's a cost.
A tax paid in tone,
a toll taken on truth.

I used to say it for others.
To ease the moment.
To finish the transaction.
To coat the silence with something everyone could
recognize.

Because for most people,
gratitude only registers
when it's wrapped in the familiar script.

And I am fluent in that script.
I know how to smile just enough.
To land the "thank you"
in the right octave—
not too rushed, not too reverent.

Sometimes I mean it.
But sometimes,
it tastes like ash.
Still, I offer it.

Not for me.
But so you don't mistake my stillness for rudeness.
So you don't take my quiet as absence.
So you don't write your own meaning
onto my unspoken one.

I still say thank you.
But mostly,
I say it to stop you from asking
if I meant it.

The WingChild

I was the kind of kid who wanted to be wherever my
dad was.
Didn't matter if it was the barbershop, the hardware
store, or just driving in circles — I wanted in.
His shadow was my dream real estate.
And to his credit, he let me tag along.
Mostly.

What he didn't say was that I wasn't tagging along
—

I was **tagged in.**
As cover.
As credibility.
As the tiny, unsuspecting co-star in a series of
morally questionable errands.

He'd make plans with me.
Big ones. Ice cream, a movie, maybe a bookstore.
Plans that sounded like fatherhood.
Plans that were believable enough to say out loud to
his wife.

And then...
"Just one stop first."
"Won't take long."

"I'll be right back."
Cue: me in the car.
Windows cracked.
Doors locked.
Nothing but my vivid imagination and a half-full
water bottle to sustain me.

Sometimes it was a bar.
Sometimes it was a shady looking apartment
complex.
Sometimes a nice one.

I wasn't scared.
I was just... confused.
And loyal.

Until I wasn't.

– – –

There was this one time — I think I was 14.
He had promised me something I was actually
excited about.
I don't remember what it was, just that it didn't
happen.
Instead, I ended up sitting awkwardly at a beachside
lunch with
— and I quote my younger self —
"some really old wrinkly white women."

I went home and told my very red-haired, very white
stepmother.
She was... not thrilled.
And neither was he.
Apparently, loyalty has conditions.
So does silence.

That may have been the beginning of the end
for believing his "plans" at face value.
I still went along sometimes.
But I brought suspicion with me.

And here's the kicker: even as I got older, the
"wingchild" gig didn't exactly retire.
No, it just upgraded.

He started bringing women around me — sometimes
under perfectly normal pretexts, sometimes not.
Like it was some covert casting call, and I was the
judge.
Did I like her?
Was she good enough?
Did she pass the "Dad's Approval" test?

If I didn't vibe with a woman he really liked, oh, he
would work to change my mind.

Hard.

Suddenly she was cooking my favorite food, learning
my favorite songs, turning into this mythical
unicorn just to get my stamp of approval.
It was less about me and more about *him* —
needing me to bless his choices so he could feel less
guilty, less exposed, less... alone in the whole mess.

– – –

Now, older and emotionally hydrated,
I look back and laugh —
but also, not really.

Because there's something quietly brutal
about being used by someone
you only ever wanted to be close to.

Even if they smiled.
Even if they meant well.
Even if, technically,
you did get to hang out with your dad.

freedom in full bloom—
but the roots feel unfamiliar
and the price, unnamed

I used to see them—
girls my age, fresh in their twenties,
spending money they didn't earn
like water with some to spare.
Hair, nails, and outfits on point.
Driving cars with tanks they never filled.
Free as birds,
fluttering from tree to tree,
catching up on the latest gossip over brunches they
didn't pay for.

Kept by men.
Sometimes one.
Sometimes more than one.
Some they reportedly didn't even have to sleep with.

And I thought—
I'm cute.
I could do that.
I deserve that freedom too.

And then my soul whispers,
"But, at what cost?"

I could spend my late nights

and even some early mornings
standing near giant speakers,
sound waves crashing through me,
energizing me—
to dance with a man I just met,
pretending I enjoy the taste of
bitter and acid.

But, at what cost?

I could script and rehearse my words like
monologues
Stand just right
to catch the best light.
Hair perfectly in place.
Nail colors to match every season.

Lean into charm.
Turn my smile into currency.
Read every room
like a market
and decide who I need to be today.

I could borrow comfort
even when it comes with strings,
even when the fine print
is printed on skin.

But, at what cost?

I could be kept,
but never still.
Seen,
but never truly known.
Chosen,
but never really safe.

But, at what cost?

some grow without scars—
how do their hearts learn thunder
without the lightning?

Did they grow up soft
because the world never asked them to harden?

Did they walk into rooms
without first shrinking?

Did they take risks
without calculating the cost
of disappointing someone
who only loved them on condition?

Did they believe in themselves
because someone else did first?

Or did they get bored—
no chaos to survive,
no wounds to explain?
Did they go looking for something to break
just to feel the shape of struggle?

Did they become
the kind of parents they had?

Did they apologize
when they were wrong—

not because they had to relearn love,
but because love taught them right?

Did they make art
without bleeding for it?
Did they sit in silence
and feel peace instead of panic?

I don't envy them.
I just wonder
who I might've been,
if someone had softened the world for me first.
If someone had called me enough
before I called myself *invisible.*

Would I have been softer?
Would I cry without apology,
and breathe without bracing for impact?
Would my shoulders sit lower,
my laugh ring cleaner,
my joy come without the taste of rust?

Would I have let people in
without planning my escape route?

Would I still write—
but *not as a survival skill?*
Would I be whole,
and not just functional?

Are the loved children thriving—
or just surviving?
Should I be grateful
that I was forged in fire instead of clouds—
because the world is not kind
and I am equipped to survive it?
Should I pity them
for not being made for this world,
or be glad they at least tasted peace?

I don't need an answer.
But I ask anyway.

Don't ask me the why.
Soul moves, then it sees.
Sometimes God speaks in draft mode.

There's a strange kind of knowing that doesn't ask
for permission.
It doesn't show up loud or labeled.
It doesn't explain itself.
It just arrives quietly... *unfinished.*

A pull to do something that doesn't yet make sense.
An urge to step left when everyone is leaning right.
An idea that feels too small to argue with,
but too persistent to ignore.

Sometimes it's a format you gravitate toward before
the world catches up.
Sometimes it's a hesitation—
to follow tradition,
to repeat the method,
to do what's always been done.
And when you try to explain it, even softly, it feels
like *speaking in parentheses.*

So you just move.
You shift the way your body is asking you to.
You say the thing in the way that feels most human.
You trade formulas for real faces.

And then—somewhere later—
a door opens behind you that looks suspiciously like
it was waiting on your footsteps to unlock.
Someone official announces what your spirit already
started practicing.
The path you wandered off to find becomes a policy.

But you're not surprised.
You're just...*still.*
Still in the same whisper you started with.
Still walking with the quiet confidence that maybe it
was never about being first—
just about being *faithful*
to the nudge,
to the *almost-thought,*
to the draft God slipped under your door
before it made it to print.

Don't Stand There, Sir.
I'm Already Wrestling Myself.

Some days, my thighs are in an underground
cage match.
No ref.
No rules.
Just unprovoked violence.
They're fighting for dominance like one's trying to
prove it's the "better leg."
I am but the referee, flinching with every step.

Meanwhile, I've been telling myself I'm not fat—
I'm just composed.
Thick with thoughts.
Heavy with potential.
Balanced, like my diet...
which includes ice cream as the calcium-rich,
dairy-adjacent, self-soothing supplement it was
clearly meant to be.

But here's where it all comes undone:

Some medieval gentleman from the era of corsets
and fainting couches
apparently taught the modern male species
to hold the door open *from inside the frame.*

Sir.

Why are you *in the doorway?*

Why is your body parallel with mine?

**Why must we share a moment
every time I try to enter a building?
Why do I have to breathe in your morning cologne
and lightly graze your chest like a timid first kiss?
Why is this a make-out session
I've been avoiding on purpose
by not choosing to date for the past 10 years?**

I didn't ask for eye contact.
I didn't sign the consent form for this architectural
seduction.

*I'm just trying to get through the door,
not the stages of intimacy.*
Not to brush clavicles with a stranger who thinks
chivalry means
turning an exit into an *experience.*

And now I have the added responsibility
of faking a smile
and coquettishly saying thank you—
like I enjoyed the chest-to-chest communion
and would recommend it to a friend.

Move, sir.

Step aside with the grace God intended when
He created vestibules.
Put the door all the way open, sir.
And back away like the gentleman your mother
hoped for.

Because I'm already fighting myself.
My thighs are in the 12th round.
And now I gotta add you to the list of obstacles
between me and my next socially acceptable breath.

Dear friend,
if the world feels too heavy,
if the walls press in,
if you're thinking about disappearing—
call me.

I'll sing to you.
Butchering your favorite songs.
Forgetting the lyrics halfway through.
Inventing my own backup vocals.
Loudly.
Off-key.
Off-tempo.
Probably off-genre.
With confidence I haven't earned.

It won't help.
Not really.

But it might make you laugh—
distracted by secondhand
embarrassment
until you forget why you were sad.

Or at least regret calling me.
Which is still better
than suffering alone.

You don't have to be okay.
You just have to remember—
I'm here.
Some people send flowers.
I send chaos,
wrapped in unconditional love.

Obedience hums—
even silence has a rank
when fear wears a name.

I wonder what part of us it is that kneels so quickly
when called.
What ancient strand in our spine hears a command
and folds,
even when the gut whispers,
"This doesn't feel right."

In the war rooms of history,
the most dangerous weapon was never the missile.
It was **belief**.
Belief that the person in charge
knew what they were doing.
Belief that your own doubt was the real enemy.

No blood on their hands—just lights on a screen.
But those lights were lives.
And the algorithm of victory
was coded in the obedience of people
who never got to ask why.

They didn't lack reason.
They lacked **permission**
to *disobey.*

And maybe that's the part that bruises me most—

that so many of us are trained for sacrifice
before we're ever taught to question it.
We're praised for **loyalty**,
not discernment.

We call it **honor**
when we offer ourselves up at the sound of a voice
just slightly louder than our own.
Even when it doesn't make sense.
Even when we know better.

And the ones who gave the order?
They call it **leadership**—
and walk away clean.

Blueprints and Red Ink

You love the idea of me.
The silhouette. The symbol. The shape that fits the empty space in your narrative.
You wanted the wife, not the woman.
The role, not the soul.
The headline, not the story.

You wanted someone who stayed home, not someone who **came alive there**.
You wanted my softness, but **not my steel**.
You wanted a lighthouse to guide you back
from your wandering —
not a mirror to make you face the ocean
inside yourself.

So you gave me **loyalty in public**, and *lies in private*.
Said all the right things with all the wrong intentions.
Chose her —
not because she was better, but because she was
easier to *disappoint*.
You could fail her without guilt.
But with me?
Failing me would be a reflection of *you*.
And you weren't ready to be seen like that.

And I couldn't even be angry...
Because once I saw the strings,
I saw the hands pulling them.

Parents do it too.
They love the idea of their child—
the blueprint they sketched in their heads before you
ever took your first breath.
But the minute you start to color outside their lines,
their "unconditional love" comes with red ink.

"What happened to my sweet little girl?"
She grew.
She learned to question the script.
She learned that being your daughter meant being
your projection —
not a person.

Even friends...
They say *"you're my ride or die"*
until you hit a bump in the road and they
let go of the wheel.
They love the way you show up for them,
but vanish when your name comes first in the
sentence.

They love how you hold space.
They do not notice how little space
they leave for you.

People don't love people.
They love versions of them.
They love utility. Aesthetic. Familiarity.
Not the burden of truth,
not the cost of presence,
not the reality of responsibility.

Because to love someone — truly —
means to meet them where they are,
without trying to drag them back to your
imagination.

So no — **you didn't love me.**
You loved the idea of me.
The clean lines. The silence. The shine.
But not the voice that challenged you.
Not the boundaries that held you accountable.
Not the weight of what I am when I'm not reduced
to your comfort.

You wanted a storybook,
but I'm a storm.
You wanted a placeholder,
but **I'm a presence.**

And if that's too much for you?
Then maybe it's not *me* you should be looking at.
Maybe it's the mirror.

Unseen hands at work—
the world runs on quiet strength,
not titles alone.

They told us to dream big.
Be the doctor, the engineer, the next tech giant.
They handed us visions of white coats and
glass offices,
and whispered that success was a *suit*,
not a uniform.

We believed them.

We studied like our lives depended on it—
because in some ways, *they did.*
Late nights, bent backs, borrowed time.
Parents working double shifts so we could one day
work indoors.
So we could be respected. Heard. Safe.

But what happens
when every child is told they must climb
and no one is taught to build the ladder?

What happens
when everyone's trying to become a doctor
but no one wants to take out the trash?

What happens to the meals served,

the beds changed,
the streets cleaned before morning traffic?
To the hands that fix the pipes,
the ones who drive the buses,
or restock the shelves
so someone else can chase their dream
uninterrupted?

We build pyramids of worth
where the base holds all the weight,
but is never given a name.

We say *dignity is in all labor*—
but only reward the labor that performs well on a
stage,
that wears a tie,
that doesn't leave grease under the fingernails.

And yet—
if every janitor stopped showing up tomorrow,
we'd all feel it
before the absence of any CEO.

We pretend ambition has one shape.
But what if success isn't *rising above* others,
but *standing solidly among them?*
What if we taught children that
there is no shame in the work that sustains a society?

That *clean water*
and *clean floors*
and *warm meals*
and *strong backs*
are not lesser dreams—
just quieter ones.

So ask yourself,
"What happens when no one wants to take out the
trash?"

She Is Not Nothing.

People are stumbling over the question:
What is a woman?
The definitions are dissolving.
The fear of offense has replaced clarity.

But maybe we've been asking the wrong question
all along.
Maybe we don't define her by what she is—
maybe we start with what she *is not.*

- - -

They ask:
What is a woman?
And the room folds in on itself.
Eyes dart, throats clear,
truth hides behind polite confusion.

Some say:
"She is *not* her womb."
"She is *not* her chromosomes."
"She is *not* her ability to mother, or bleed,
or soften the sharp edges of a world built by men."

So if a woman is *not* these,

then what *is* she?

We are told—
She is whoever says she is.
She is a claim.
A costume.
A story.
A vibe.

But language is not a mood.
It requires edges.
Definitions.
Limits.

So let's ask it differently.

What is *not* a woman?
What stands across from her
in the mirror of meaning?

A man, maybe.
An unbent tree, rooted in the word *no.*
Broad shoulders taught never to cry.
Voice two octaves deeper,
expectations five bricks higher.
A history of conquest. A suit. A war. A wage.

Not a woman is
an origin not shaped to receive.

A body that was told from birth
to act, not *become.*
A life rarely interrupted
by the need to shrink or justify.
A default setting.

And so,
if one leaves that identity—
lays down the sword,
undoes the collar,
steps out of the assumption—
do they arrive at "*woman*"?
Or do they arrive at *not-man?*

Because these are not the same.

Not a woman is
not simply what you *take off,*
but what you *step into*—
what wraps itself around your bones
when no one's looking.

Not a woman is
not a slur, not a judgment—
but a *boundary.*
A *map.*
A line that tells us where language still holds shape.

If we can no longer say what a woman *is,*

perhaps we must begin
by remembering what she is *not.*

Not a man.
Not a metaphor.
Not a maybe.
Not a blank page where anything goes.

A woman may be many things.
But she is *not nothing.*

And if she is *not nothing* —
then she must be *something.*
Let us start there.

Make Me Believe

You want to be heard,
but your voice is *paper-thin*—
a whisper in a crowded train,
flattened by the rhythm of louder feet.

Speak all the truth you want.
Paint it in gold,
lace it with light,
wrap it in ribbon and righteousness—
if you do not *hold the room,*
the room will *not hold you.*

Command us.
Not with ego,
but with *presence*—
a voice that doesn't *ask* for space,
but *takes it,*
like breath after silence.

And if not that,
be the one who makes us laugh.
Disarm us with charm,
with eyes that *twinkle* when you talk,
with timing that lands like a *wink*
between syllables.

I don't need theatrics.
I don't need perfect cadence.
I need substance.
I need you to *sit in your message*
like it came from your own bones.

Make me believe
that what you're saying
you actually *believe yourself.*

Speak plainly if you must.
Speak gently, if that's your gift.
But *don't pretend.*

If you offer only purity,
only goodness,
only the gentle weight
of well-meaning—
no matter how noble your cause—
if it doesn't light you up,
it won't reach me.

I will *drift.*
Not because you're wrong.
But because you've left
no *gravity*
to hold me there.
And I don't owe my attention
to someone who hasn't even given
their own.

Called from the Waist Down

I was building an empire—
Monopoly board stretched wide,
money stacked,
lip curled just enough
to signal I was *not here to lose.*

The blue Nokia brick was wedged somewhere
between my *principles* and my *pelvic bone,*
forgotten
in the heat of hostile takeovers
and property wars.

And then—

A vibration from the gods
or the devil himself.
Not a sound, just
a jolt to the root
of my being.

My hand froze mid-card.
My gaze locked with a boy
who did nothing wrong

except exist
at *ground zero.*

My eyes screamed,
"Do you feel this too?"
His replied,
"Should I call someone?"

The room went still.
I sat there,
an *unmoving boss with a secret*
trembling throne.

I excused myself
with all the dignity one can carry
while secretly being called
by *her own crotch.*

In the bathroom,
truth revealed itself:
Nokia.
Face down.
Vibrating like a traitor
on silent mode.

I returned,
straightened my spine,
and bought three hotels.

bare feet on the floor
emotional hurricane
steadfast in the calm

I will stomp into your peace *barefoot and dramatic.*
I will throw words like darts **dipped in old trauma**,
look you in the eye like it's your fault
I *didn't nap today,*
then demand a cuddle while I sob into your
collarbone
about a TikTok I can't even explain.

Don't flinch.

You knew what this was.

Let me unravel.
Let me yell about something **symbolic**
that's not really about you but also
definitely about you.
Let me test your structure with *emotional wind*
and make sure you can still hold me when I finally
collapse.

Drag me, yes—
but gently.
With the calm of a man
who's seen hurricanes with lipstick before.

Block my chaos,
not my voice.
Catch the vase I didn't mean to throw.
Sit beside my storm,
and then—
be the thunder *louder than mine.*

And when I kick you emotionally,
don't lecture me.
Don't shrink.
Don't snap.

Just win.

Win my trust with your *silence.*
Win my surrender with your *steadiness.*
Win my respect by **never asking me to be smaller**
just to keep you comfortable.

Because I will come back.
Every time.
After the storm.
With tea and a blanket
and a half-apology in the form of *forehead kisses* and
unsolicited foot rubs.

I don't need perfection.
Just presence.
Just someone who doesn't flinch

when the drama is homemade
and the villain is PMS.

You can lead me.
You can check me.

But baby—

**you better drag me gently
while I kick you emotionally.**

I asked one question.
Got dreams, avocados, tears.
The group heard a vibe.

I used to think if I just worded things
clearly enough,
people would respond in kind.
Turns out, people don't respond to what you said.
They respond to *whatever they felt like hearing.*

You ask a group:
"What stood out to you from this week's reading?"
and somehow, you get
a side story about someone's neighbor,
a 10-minute tangent about *avocados*,
and a tearful memory from the 90s.

People just *sprint away* from the actual question
and then stare at you like *you're* the weird one
when you say:
"...That's not what I asked."

So eventually, someone tried to fix it.
Made the question more *"open,"* more
"accommodating."
Added options:
"...about the main theme, a character,
or anything else."
And boom—suddenly it's back to:

"Page 34 really spoke to me."
Like we didn't just survive verbal jazz improv
for three weeks straight.

I sat there thinking—what kind of logic is this?!
When the question was specific, they improvised.
When it got vague, they snapped to attention.
Are we dealing with humans
or reverse psychology experiments?

And then I realized—
It's not stupidity.
It's group behavior.

Give most people too much clarity,
and they'll look for a side door.
Give them vagueness with a clipboard vibe,
and they'll follow the imaginary rules.

This is why I no longer argue with interpretation.
If I say something and you decide to rewrite it in
your head—
That's between you and your imagination.
I'm not chasing your feelings around the room
like they're loose chickens.

I've made peace with this strange species
we live among.
But please don't tell me I need to learn how to
communicate.

I've been speaking clearly this whole time.
Y'all just keep bringing riddles
to a conversation.

They say, *"I had no choice"*—
as if hard options mean no options at all.
As if survival requires erasing the truth
of **choosing it.**

But the gun didn't pull the trigger for you.
Your fear didn't force your hand.
The world didn't stop spinning
until you said yes.

You made the choice—
to live,
to fight,
to protect or betray,
to let someone else fall.

You could have chosen to die.
You didn't.
And I respect that.

But don't pretend you were swept away
by a wave you didn't step into.

You chose.
Now honor it.
And carry the weight.

The Punch was Too Sweet

I don't drink.
Not for religious reasons, not for shame—
just because I like to know **who's steering the ship**
when my body decides to speak.

So when my sister handed me that cup—
sweet, fruity, festive—
I didn't think twice.
Just smiled, sipped, and said yes
to another.

By cup three, we're mid-game,
someone's shouting *Uno*,
and suddenly my thighs are sending up
smoke signals
from somewhere *ancient and below.*

Heat bloomed.
Every cell between my hips whispered,
"Are we... are we doing this now?"
My face said *poker*,
but my pelvis said *panic.*
Something inside me unlocked
and peeked around the corner like,
"Heeeey stranger."

I asked, *quietly*,
"Is there alcohol in this?"
And they lied.
Smiled.
Said *no*.
Kept dancing.

I put the cup down
like it had *teeth*.
And kept moving like nothing happened
—except I was now *learning Beyoncé choreo*
and apparently, *having a great time.*

At the end of the night,
my sister confessed.
**"Just a splash. You're always so serious.
We wanted to be sure you'd have fun."**

Like my boundaries
were just *inconvenient tupperware*
they couldn't pry open
without heat.

I laughed.
But made a note.

Next time I sip sweetness
and my body sings before the music starts—
I'll trust the tune.

Eyes half-closed, I smile
they call me weird, but better
than the yelling kind

They say I used to enter like mist — soundless, slow, the way comfort creeps into a cold room. One used to laugh about it, telling others how I'd glide in at dawn just to press a quiet kiss on a sleeping back like an affectionate ninja. A grown man, they'd say, not a baby — but somehow I never got that memo. I wasn't waking a person, I was greeting the day... gently, with affection, like it deserved a soft launch. He would groan like a bear waking from hibernation, and I'd scamper off before his ego could recover.

Another voice — bright, strange, beloved — liked to drag me from dreams just to share whatever cosmic chaos had bloomed in her brain. Aliens disguised as Uber drivers. A theory about how toast is proof we live in a simulation. A business plan involving goats and glitter. I'd blink awake mid-dream, see her eyes shining, and somehow smile. Listening. Ready. Like I'd been waiting just for this moment. And really— who wouldn't want to be greeted by joy, dressed in madness. It always made me wonder: why do people romanticize rage in the morning? Loud alarms, grunts, groans, rolled eyes?

Isn't peace the more radical entrance?

You've been
handing out roses—
kindness, wisdom, beauty,
like petals from your palms—
hoping no one looks too closely
at the garden they came from.

Hoping they don't see
the weeds still tangled in the soil.
The ones you've tried to pull
a dozen times.
The ones *with names.*
With *histories.*
With *roots.*

But even weeds grow in sunlight.
Even messes hold fragrance.
And maybe you've forgotten—
the roses came from that same dirt.

The bloom and *the buried*
are both you.

You're not hiding weakness.
You're living through it—
and still offering beauty anyway.

I carried her weight
and still she said she was left—
grief cannot see hands.

She said, *"No one cares about me. No one does
anything for me,"*
with such conviction—such *finality*—that I froze.
I blinked a few times, turned on my heels,
and walked away like a ghost.

I didn't visit, call, or speak to her for months.
Because in that moment, I couldn't reconcile
what she said
with everything I had just done.

I didn't know yet what I know now:
That when people are *drowning in their own trauma—
neck-deep in pain they can't name or hold—*
they say foolish things,
like *Job blaming God for his ruin.*
They can't see the good.
Even when it's standing in front of them, *arms full.*
Even when it's love, *disguised as groceries and
shoulder-pressed water jugs.*

But here's the thing:
Just because they *can't see it*
doesn't mean it doesn't *hurt like hell*

to be erased from their version of events.

She said, *"No one cares about me. No one does*
anything for me,"
as I set down the five-gallon bottle
I carried in for her.
As I handed her the last of the money
I'd squirreled away
for her laundry.
After I'd been slapped in the face for lying
to my boyfriend
about where the rest of it went—because he didn't
want me
supporting her.

Sometimes you don't know
the flames someone walked through,
the coals they crossed barefoot,
just to hand you
one quiet moment of peace.

I wanted her to focus on school.
To not have to choose between scraps and abuse.
I tried to be her shelter.

But I couldn't give her
what the other girls had—
the soft life, the shopping bags,
the comfort bought by men twice their age.

She wanted *ease*.
She wanted *safety*.
I get that now.

But even *understanding*
doesn't keep a heart from bleeding
when it's been split by the very hands
it was trying to feed.

hands moved in silence
threading meaning into form
then someone spoke loud

Weaving?
Women spun thread from their bare hands,
dyed it with soil and berries,
wove patterns into memory —
not for applause,
but because their families were cold.
Centuries pass.
A man picks up a loom and suddenly—
"Textile Artist."

Childcare?
A woman raises four children,
feeds them from her body,
soothes tantrums, tempers, trauma.
No wage. No pension.
A man wears a baby carrier in public once
and goes viral.
"Super Dad."
"TikTok Hero."
"Heartwarming."

Home décor?
A woman rearranges furniture for flow and peace.
"She's nesting."
"She has too much time."

A man buys a ladder shelf and hangs three black-
and-white prints—
**"Visionary. Minimalist King.
You should see his loft."**

Healing?
Women crushed herbs *before Google.*
Whispered prayers over the sick.
Brought life into this world with bare hands and
blood-soaked linens.
Then men gave it Latin names, wrote it in books,
outlawed the women who taught them,
and crowned themselves **Doctors.**

**Women build.
Men brand.**
And the world
only claps
when he does it.

Why They Clap for Me

I hung a fern and called it *balance.*
You staged a home,
matched colors to emotion,
and no one noticed.

You fed a child for ten years.
I packed a lunch *once*,
and they asked me for tips.

I watched a YouTube video,
tried your grandmother's recipe,
burned the bottom —
but brought it to the office anyway.
Now they call me Chef.

I stitched together secondhand denim
for an art show.
They paid me five grand
for a story your mother lived
and never once sold.

I use *your* language
in my TED Talk
about **"empathy in leadership."**
They gave me a standing ovation.

You said it first —
in a meeting they talked over.

I don't even lie.
I just *arrive.*
Do what you've done for free
with lights on me,
and they call it **genius.**

I'm not better.
I'm just seen.

Reader discretion advised:
This piece may cause sudden clarity.

There must be *something* in the water.
That's the only way to explain it.

How else do you account for a culture
where a middle schooler knows
she's invisible unless she's holding
a **$60 thermos**?
Where friendships have brand names
and kindness has a retail price?

There must be *something* in the food.
Because nowhere else do people
march into grocery stores
and out of classrooms
with the same kind of **casual violence**.

And yes—
there is violence in other countries.
People are being **silenced**.
Exploited.
Bullied.
Erased.
They are dying too.
But not like this.
Not with such **absurdity**.

Not over **memes and mugs**.
Not because someone missed their morning
serotonin spike
from *likes* and blind allegiance.

It's not just the sugar.
Not just the hormones.
Not just the **processed loneliness**
wrapped in plastic and sold by aisle number.

No.
It's the **media**.
It's the never-ending stream of *suggestion*
whispered by **screens that never sleep**.
You are not enough.
You are not beautiful.
You are not safe—
unless you buy this, believe this, fear this.

There must be *something* in the signal.
Because only here can a person
consume trauma as entertainment
and wake up the next day to reenact it
for views.

Only here can a child raise themselves
on *chaos, calories, and curated content*
while their parents drown in
debt, distraction, and

"did you see what happened in the news?"

There must be *something* in the culture.
Because somehow the **richest country on earth**
has citizens with *nothing to say*
unless it's **screamed, filtered, or monetized.**
And somehow the **freest country on earth**
can't tell the difference between
freedom and a **free fall**.

So yes—
there must be *something* in the water.
Because what else explains a place
where a man can lose his job
for sharing an Elmo-on-a-toilet meme
and a child can lose her life
for going to school?

Whatever it is,
it seeps through the food, the phones,
the families—
until you *forget*
you were ever **whole**.

And the only ones scared
of someone else
running the algorithm
are the ones who already know
they broke their own.

deep tide keeps secrets —
small lights bob and look away;
I hold my own pulse.

I've walked through life with open eyes,
expecting arms where there were only *shadows*.
Never fooled by *kindness wrapped in absence*,
or *warmth that never touched my bones.*

They mistook my *silence* for *softness*,
my *clarity* for *threat*.
All I offered was **presence**—
unflinching, unperformed—
and they blinked as if light hurt their eyes.

I used to ache for love
like a child who keeps checking the *horizon*—
sure it would come if I stayed *good*,
if I stayed *bright*.
But some hearts only bloom in shallow soil,
and I—
I was planted deep.

No one poured into me without trying to
drain me,
as if my soul were a well they forgot to *refill*.
They came to *take*,
not to *see*.

And still—
I do not burn.
I do not beg.
I simply stand,
steady in my knowing.

Because what I wanted was never *attention*,
it was **recognition**.
Not the *theatre of care,*
but its *quiet pulse*—
that rare, wordless answering
you **cannot fake, cannot forge, cannot force**.

I have met no one who could hold me there—
not family, not lover, not friend.
So **I held myself**,
and in that holding,
I have never been alone.

I stopped asking the sea to understand
mountains.
Stopped handing mirrors to those who fear
reflection.
I made peace with the *stillness of waiting*—
for a resonance that may never come.

Because I wasn't made for shallow waters,
and I **will not drown myself**
so someone else can say *they saw me.*

You say you always loved me.

But I searched the minutes and the messages.
The *missed calls.*
The *milestones*.
The moments where I stood alone
hoping you'd arrive
or at least explain why you didn't.

And you didn't.

– – –

You say you always loved me.

But *where was it?*

Was it hiding under all that silence?
Was it buried in the busyness,
tucked between errands and ego?

Because I checked the texts.
I checked the dates.

I checked the ache in my own body
where your *name lived rent-free*
but your hands never showed up to hold
anything real.

– – –

You see, **love has fingerprints.**

It leaves *trails*.
It *shows up*.
Even when it's tired.
Even when it's not convenient.
Especially then.

– – –

You say you always loved me.

But love is not what disappears
when things get complicated.
It is not what stands in the back row of your life
while you perform kindness for strangers
and offer nothing but memory to me.

You say you always loved me.

But love does *not* miss entire years.
It does *not* dodge phone calls
like they owe it money.
It does not spend generously on
temporary people
while those it birthed go hungry.

It does not ask to be understood
before it's ever made an effort to *understand*.

– – –

You say you always loved me.

But I don't remember love
being this *cold*.
This *absent*.
This *selective*.

I don't remember love
asking for forgiveness
with the same mouth
that never once asked
if I was okay.

If this is love,
then love must have *amnesia.*
Because I was there.
Waiting.
Reaching.
Calling.
Explaining.
Covering.
Forgiving.
Surviving.

And you—
you were somewhere else,
telling yourself
that *thinking of me from a distance*
was enough.

It wasn't.

You say you always loved me.

But love isn't just a *feeling.*
It's a *footprint.*
And you never walked far enough
in my direction to leave one.

Domestic Decoys

There is a bird—*don't ask me which,*
I'm not a zoologist—
but he's small, he's blue, and he does this wildly
unnecessary mating dance.

He puffs up like a microwave marshmallow, flares
his feathers in a halo, and dodges from side to side
like he's trying to fake out a ghost linebacker.
The female watches—eyes wide, brain buffering—
clearly wondering whether she's being seduced or
auditioned for an improv group.
And before she can decide...
he mates.
Done.
No refunds.

I'm convinced this is exactly what modern men are
doing with... cooking.

And cleaning.

And folding the fitted sheet like it's not the most
infernal object known to humanity.

It's the same hypnotic distraction. A sleight of hand.

They flash competence.
They sauté onions like they've been simmering in self-awareness.
They vacuum like they're clearing the path to your heart.
They load the dishwasher like they're emotionally available.
And you—bless your soul—you start to think:
Maybe I've found the one.

You didn't.

You found a man who can julienne vegetables with military precision
but emotionally clocks out at *"I don't like conflict."*
You found a human IKEA catalog who can deep-clean a bathroom
but treats accountability like a virus he's dodging.
You found a man who builds furniture without instructions
but can't tell you how he feels without bursting into smoke.

You think you've struck gold because he knows the difference between a sauté pan and a skillet.
But that's not intimacy.
That's choreography.

It's a mating ritual.

And you, my dear, are the bedazzled bird.

This is how they get us.
With freshly baked bread.
With hand-wiped counters.
With *"Look babe, I alphabetized the spices."*

And the next thing you know, you're in a
relationship
where you're still the one doing the emotional labor,
the mental scheduling,
the conflict mediation,
and the inner child reparenting—
except now you feel guilty for complaining because
he cooks.
And you've never been with a man who cooks.

It's not that we don't appreciate the effort.
It's that the effort stops at the surface.
The show ends when the stove cools.

So no, I'm not impressed anymore.
Not unless you can also name your emotions without
a flashcard.
Not unless you can say *"I was wrong"* without
collapsing.
Not unless you clean the emotional kitchen too.

Because I've learned something now:
It's not that rare for a man to cook.
The real miracle
is one who can sit in silence with your
pain
and not try to fix it with food,
but *feel it with you*
until it passes.

youth shamed into dust —
now we dance in what we missed,
aging out of fear.

I was sixteen.
We laughed at them—pointed fingers,
twisted brows,
Whispered loudly like they couldn't hear.
Because they dared to wear pigtails,
Baggy jeans, crop tops, and sneakers.
We shamed them into conforming.
Dressed them like eighty-year-old grandmas
With bobs, tweeds below the knees, crossed ankles—
Like they should be bouncing second generations on
their laps,
Offering freshly baked cookies.
They were only thirty. Forty.

And you don't know what it's like
Until it is you—
Until you wake up one day
To gray hairs and lines
You swear weren't there yesterday.
Because inside, you still feel nineteen.

You don't know what it's like
To have your childhood—
Twenty years of your life—
Stolen from you.

Clothes you should've worn,
Places you should've gone,
Experiences you should've had.

You don't know what it feels like
To look into the faces of your children—
To see the people around you,
With the pieces seemingly in place—
And still feel like you've never lived.

Why do you want to take more from them?
Isn't it enough?
Let them dance hip hop at forty,
Become authors at fifty,
Fall in love again
Or for the first time at 60
Bodybuilders at seventy.

Who are you
To decide how this soul expresses itself,
How it celebrates this gift of life?

I was you.
And now—
I know what it feels like too.

The World:
You are **mother.**
You are **wife.**
You are the **root** we plant ourselves in.

The Woman:
And what grows from me
has **swallowed my name.**
Did you ever ask
if I wanted to be *soil?*

The World:
You are **sacred sacrifice.**
You are the reason we **live.**

The Woman:
Then why do I feel like a **ghost**
haunting my own *heartbeat?*
Why can't I remember
if I liked **polka dots** or **stripes?**

The World:
We thought you didn't need
such things anymore.

The Woman:
But they were **mine**.
Tiny, bright pieces
of who I was
before I was **yours**.

The World:
You are **man.**
You are **provider.**
You are the **pillar** we build our lives on.

The Man:
And holding everyone up
has **hollowed me out.**
Did you ever ask
if I wanted to be *stone?*

The World:
You are **strength.**
You are the reason we **stand.**

The Man:
Then why do I feel like an **empty house**
echoing with *other people's voices?*
Why can't I remember
the sound of my own **laughter**
when no one is watching?

The World:
We thought a man like you
should have *outgrown* such things.

The Man:
But they were **mine.**
Not grand. Not loud.
Just the *unguarded moments*
where I could lay my armor down
and still be **me.**

Borrowed Grace

There's this dancer on YouTube. A Chinese man with wrists like calligraphy and feet that don't so much move as *glide through dimensions.* He does this jazz fusion—modern, traditional, mysterious—like someone taught him choreography *in a dream* and he just woke up remembering every step *with feeling.*

He's not just doing dance. *He is dance.* His neck rolls could narrate bedtime stories. His pinky alone has better rhythm than most people's hips. If a move calls for a head dip, he gives you a trilogy: shoulder rolls, a neck poem, then—*snap!*—the head drops like the curtain on opening night.

And behind him? A row of beautiful women hitting every step. *Perfectly. Rigidly.* Emotionless as a tax form. They've got all the gear—lashes, ponytails, flawless postures—but next to him, it's like watching mannequins moonwalk. You could replace them with coat racks and the show would lose nothing but hair flips.

It made me uncomfortable, honestly. As a woman, I've been told *I am grace.*

That it lives in my hips, my lashes, the sway of my walk. *I've inherited it, apparently.* But watching this man swirl his wrist with the sorrow of a thousand years while his backup dancers blinked through the choreography like elegant placeholders—*there to hold space, not steal it*—I started asking questions.

Like: *when did we start thinking being seen as a woman was enough?*
When did we decide femininity could rest on autopilot while we lip-sync through life with borrowed hair and high heels?

He didn't steal our grace. *He earned it.*

Meanwhile, we're out here assuming estrogen equals elegance and forgetting that presence—*real, embodied, intentional presence*—has no gender.

So yeah, I laughed. But it was the kind of laugh that carried a little shame and a little awe.

Because if grace can be learned, if it can live in a man's wrist and neck and spine—
then girl, we've got work to do.

How rude of him, though—
to out-grace a room of girls
with just one neck roll.
I stood in my softest skin
still thinking that was enough.

The Further You Climb

They say **wealth buys freedom**, but sometimes it
only buys *distance*.
The further you climb, the harder it is to see the
ground.
Hunger becomes a story in the news,
thirst becomes a statistic on a chart.
Suffering blurs into something abstract,
easier to glance at than to face.

But for those who live with less, compassion is never
abstract.
It's in the *empty bowl* passed across the table,
in the *funeral fund* raised by neighbors who barely
have rent,
in the *last bit of rice* offered to a friend
because they know what it feels like to go without.

It is the people who can least afford to give
who understand giving the most.
Because **empathy is not born from abundance —**
it is born from proximity.
Scarcity teaches you the sound of another person's
hunger;
wealth teaches you how to insulate yourself from it.

If those at the top carried the *urgency of the dying*,
the world could turn overnight.
But compassion does not always scale with income.
Sometimes, **it shrinks with it.**

And so the world turns on its head:
those who have nothing give everything,
while those who could make the greatest difference
find new ways to spend on themselves.

What He Need Money For?

Let's be real.

If the bills are paid,
the fridge is full,
the Wi-Fi works,
the socks are hole-free,
and you got clean underwear folded in drawers
you didn't even open—

What you need money for, sir?

No, really.
What is the purpose?

You got a packed lunch.
Your favorite lotion restocked.
That one snack you like that's always
mysteriously refilled
even though you "don't remember finishing it."
I know.
I know everything.

I paid your gym membership six months in advance
so your *"wellness journey"* stays funded

and nobody has to hear about protein powder again.

You got your little pocket money
for haircuts, bubble tea, and two beers
with your boys.
Maybe three, if y'all tip cheap.

That's your fun fund.
Your *"outside"* allowance.

So again... what else you need money for?

You need new shoes?
I already bought them.
You just didn't open the other box behind the one
you always reach for.

You want a new hoodie?
That's wild, because one's arriving Thursday.
In your favorite color.
On sale.
*Because I'm not just your woman—I'm your discount
oracle.*

- - -

So when a man starts mumbling about
"needing a separate account,"

or "just wanting some financial independence,"
my eyebrow lifts like rent in a gentrified
neighborhood.

Because *why?*

Where are you going?
What are you planning?
What are you trying to buy
that your wife shouldn't already know about?

Let me guess.
It's not groceries.
It's not socks.
It's not a new pillow.
It's *definitely* not toilet paper.

So again I ask:

What.
You.
Need.
Money.
For?

Because listen—
when a man ain't got financial mystery,
he ain't got emotional mischief.

And if your life is so cared for
that even your stress is on a predictable schedule,
you better hold my hand and sit down somewhere.

Love doesn't just cook.
It budgets.
It plans.
It notices when your sneakers start to lean
to the side
and your favorite pants getting tired in the knees.

So unless you trying to surprise me
with a diamond-studded goat or a deed to the moon,

don't insult this sacred spreadsheet union
by acting like you need a secret wallet.

Because let's be honest,
you ain't buying freedom.
You buying trouble.

I got the home.
I got the socks.
I got your back.

Now sit down and finish your meal prep.
You're welcome.

Thoughts of darkness
but also thoughts of light
I am neither of these
but also all of these
I am not my thoughts
and *neither are you.*

Anger kicks chairs.
Slams doors.
Writes long texts in all caps,
Then unsends them for moral superiority.

Anger still wants to be heard.
Wants to fix it.
Wants to throw lightning just to prove it's still
storming.

But **Disappointment**...
Disappointment doesn't raise its voice.
It folds the stage curtain.
Turns off the mic.
And leaves the theater before the final act.

You're not center stage anymore.
You're not **even in the room.**
The ushers are stacking chairs,
and I'm halfway home in flats,
already forgetting your last line.

See, **anger** means I'm still in it.
Still circling the wound,
checking if it bleeds.

But **disappointment**—
that's me deleting your character
from the entire script.

Not out of hate.
Not even spite.
Just... **clarity.**

The kind that tastes like still water.
The kind that doesn't need applause.

some lights turn on slow—
*as if waiting for someone
to say they deserve it*

It's an odd thing,
to pass through your 20s
not feeling ugly exactly—
just... *unattractive*.
Like the world never noticed you were there.
Like your features forgot to arrive on time
and never apologized for the delay.

Growing up, they teased you,
not because you were broken—
but because you were *unfinished*.
You didn't really have a face until twelve.
Not a bad one.
Just *not yet*.

You call it your **Stone Face Period**,
like the guy from *Fantastic Four*—
everything technically present,
but pooled like unset clay.
Eyes like lazy fabric slits,
a nose bridge *missing in action*
(a medical miracle how one ever grew in later),
and a face shaped like a baking pan—
round, wide, innocent to the cruelty
of defined jawlines

and sisters with cinematic silhouettes.

And then—
one day—
you *popped.*
Like a pregnancy belly.
Twelve hit, and your features arrived
like guests late to a surprise party.

Suddenly, men hovered.
And mirrors gave confusing answers.
The before and after versions of you
looked *almost* the same—
but the world responded **differently**.

And now—
you scroll through old photos
where you once felt misplaced in your own skin
and catch yourself saying:
"Wait. Who's that girl?"

A cutie pie.
In the sky.
Already glowing—
long before the world admitted it.

You wonder now,
how many people were quietly
drawn to you,
and how many mirrors
you were robbed of
just because your beauty
didn't arrive on cue.

wolves wear many skins—
some with sparkle, some with lace
all of them are warm.

I remember when I used to sit through
Lifetime movies like church.
Tuned in to pain like it was programming.
Watching women fall apart over and over again, and
somehow
I didn't get tired of it.
I mourned for them.
Even when I didn't have words for why.

But something else grew too—
a quiet ache in my chest,
a tension between the *empathy* I felt
and the *hatred* I started to notice
woven into the scripts.
Not mine—**but theirs.**

The men were always monsters.
The women always prey.
Every story the same: *He was watching her.*
He followed her.
He ruined her.
And we kept tuning in.

Even as a kid, I wondered—
if we fear being seen so much,

why do we draw maps to our bodies and call it
fashion?
Why is a bikini "cute" and underwear *"shameful,"*
when they're made from the same thread?
Why are we told to express ourselves freely,
but then expected to collapse
when someone takes that freedom the wrong way?

Where's the line?
And why are we the only ones punished for not
knowing it?

It burns me now.
We cry for the children harmed by predators
and then parade our own kids in crop tops
and mini skirts
to the applause of strangers.
We clutch our pearls over abuse
but raise our sons and daughters on
double standards,
likes, filters, and denial.

We say *"no means no"*
and it should.
But this world does not run on *should*.
It runs on **opportunity**.
On **impulse**.
On **power**.

So why are we still pretending it doesn't?

Why are we still dressing for innocence
in a world that has shown us time and again
that it devours the soft and the unaware?

I'm not saying **shame your skin**.
I'm saying **protect your soul**.

Because when it happens—
the betrayal, the violation, the aftermath—
you are the one who has to live with it.
Not the system.
Not the strangers.
Not the screenwriters.
You.

So no—
I don't think it's *cute* anymore.
I don't think *"let them be free"* means
"let them be bait."
I don't think awareness is paranoia.
I think it's **love**.

Hard love.
But **real**.

i spent hours curating the front—
smoothed edges, balanced tones,
a softness just sharp enough
to be taken seriously.
every glance rehearsed.
every word weighed.

but no one ever told me
how wild i looked from behind.
how the wind played with strands
i forgot to pin,
how shadows pooled in the folds of my walk.
they saw pieces i didn't know i'd left exposed.

i am a thousand choices,
edited for symmetry—
yet still misread
by angles *i can't reach.*

there's a silence
between *what i meant*
and *what they heard.*
a distance between
how i enter a room
and *what lingers after i've gone.*

and maybe that's the truth of it—
we are all **portraits**
with blurred corners,
known in fractions,
loved in translation.

not because we're hiding—
but because even the loudest soul
can't echo in every direction.

When Thank You Stopped Tasting Right

I started saying *"I appreciate you"*
because **thank you** stopped feeling true.

It got overused,
flattened,
pressed into politeness until it was *too thin to carry weight.*

So I reached for something with more soul in it.

"I appreciate you"
doesn't just acknowledge what you did—
it **honors who you are.**
It places the *being* before the *doing.*

And the first time I said it out loud,
I felt the difference.
It landed fuller in the air.
It made people pause.

They didn't always know how to respond.
But some did.
They heard the intention tucked behind the words—
the slower heartbeat,
the eye contact that came with it.

And once,
he said it back.
No hesitation. No mimicry.
He meant it.
And I knew in that moment:
he got it.
He'd felt the shift.

So I kept using it.
Not for show.
Not for trend.
Just... because it fit.
Because it had flavor again.
Because it came from the same place
the gratitude lived.

I don't need to be thanked
in order to feel appreciated.
But if you're going to say something,
make it true.

Let There Be Cotton

There is a **sacredness** to fabric.
A reverence in threads.
A *ministry* in even the humblest tank top
that keeps a man from crossing the invisible line
between **shirtless** and
naked-naked.

Not sensual.
Not sculptural.
Just... *exposed.*
Like he peeled his skin off with his hoodie
and forgot to tuck the humanity back in.

Some men carry their torsos like **gospel**—
a *soft-spoken sermon of sun-kissed abs* and quiet
confidence.
Others?
They walk into frame with **no shirt and no shame,
glowing like uncooked chicken**
and *flesh-lit trauma.*
And we are not okay.

It's not about **lust.**
It's not even about **decency.**
It's about **visual consent.**

The *silent agreement* that when you enter the chat,
you will **not** look
like an anatomy textbook
just opened to the muscle fibers
without warning.

I once loved a man like this—
beautiful in face, in spirit, in voice.
But the second that shirt came off,
my soul recoiled
like it had been shown something
unhealable.

He didn't need judgment.
He needed **intervention.**
So I praised the **fabric.**
I left glowing comments on **cotton appearances.**
I cheered for **linen.**
I whispered sweet affirmations
to every *stitched sleeve,*
hoping they'd stay loyal.

Because listen—
when your chest tone
looks like **trauma in 4K,**
when your nipples scream
"I'm unseasoned but emotionally raw,"
then yes, sir,
I need you to put it back on.

Let there be **cotton**.
Let there be **mercy**.
Let there be **modesty**
for the *mole-rat-shouldered*
men
who mean well
but forgot
that not every torso was
meant for daylight.

And if you see me in the
comments,
applauding *a tasteful hoodie?*
Just know—
I am doing the Lord's work.

violence withheld—
the calmest hands often hold
the sharpest stories

I am the worst person to argue with.
Because I will not give you fire.
You can come with teeth bared, eyes blazing—
and I will tilt my head, curious,
offering you a seat and a glass of water.

I don't meet rage with rage.
Not because I am soft,
but because **I have tasted what my rage can do.**
And *I do not play with it.*

Even in high betrayal,
I'm the one trying to help you understand
why you're angry
so you can say it better.

You—dragon.
Me—dragon therapist.

I don't enter rooms with the intention to control.
But I could,
and that's why I don't.
Because anger, when I allow it,
feels too much like **purpose.**
Too much like **prophecy.**

Too much like a **duty** I could carry out
without flinching.

And that's the thing.
I don't rage.
Because I could ruin.

Even the girl
who indefinitely borrowed
the boy I gave myself to—
called me often,
updated me on their wandering love story.
And I?
I answered.
Listened.
Asked questions.

Not because I am a fool.
But because **I wanted to understand**
how someone becomes
the kind of person
who needs to do that.

Because *I am disturbing.*
I don't see a person as one thing.
I see the string of their becoming—
the layers, the wounds,
the thousand paper cuts that made them.
I don't excuse it.

But I see it.

Even violence.
Even violation.
I could see how it's made,
what ingredients went into the hand that harms.
That doesn't mean I justify it.
It means **I watch for the recipe
so I don't accidentally become it.**

There was a scene once—
a man, desperate,
blood seeping under the door
as he slammed his body into it.
And I said,
without flinching:
"Beautiful."

And it was.
Because sometimes suffering and love
look the same
when framed by intention.

I am the best and worst person to marry.
I don't love possessively.
If one day you want to roam,
go.

I won't stop you.
Just don't touch me again.
And **don't bring disease**
into the house I keep clean.

I won't scream.
I won't break things.
But I will speak
in a voice so calm
it will feel like judgment.

I will cook.
Clean.
Even nurse you if you fall ill.
But your body will become **memory.**
Nothing more.

Because I've never leaned into anger.
Because I know
that if I ever did...

I wouldn't need to raise my voice.
I'd just pick up the knife
and set the table.

No one calls me mother.
And still,
I am whole.

I was born with a stillness
most mistook for *shyness*.
But it was **knowing**—
that the world was *too loud*
for the way I listened.

I didn't run toward the crowd.
I *watched it pass like weather.*
Felt the ache of strangers,
the heartbreak of dogs,
the echo of children
before they could even speak it.

They say the womb is made to *hold*,
but my arms have only ever reached
for *silence*,
for *sky*,
for the kind of **peace**
that doesn't ask to be named.

Yes—
I love children.
Their *giggles*.
Their *chaos*.
Their soft, sudden *wisdom*.

But I could never bear
to watch their light dim in a world
I can't protect them from.
And that love,
that raw, *unshielded* love—
was too *holy to gamble*
on my own longing.

So I chose
a *different motherhood.*
Of **pages.**
Of **moments**.
Of *memories no one will inherit*
but me.

And now,
the question arrives
not like thunder,
but like dusk:

**Will I wish I had a name
someone whispered
after I'm gone?**

**Will my silence
be mistaken for
regret?**

But *listen*—
Not all hearts are *hollowed*
by what they don't carry.

Some are **shaped**
by the *mercy*
of what they chose
not to hold.

the roof still stands tall
but inside, the walls are dust—
love was never loud

When did the prize become the burden?
When did the dream become *debt*—
to be paid in silence,
in swallowed feelings,
in children raised by ghosts of men
who sit in the living room
but haven't been *present* in years?

They say a man provides.
As if *money* makes a home.
As if handing over a paycheck
is the same as *holding your child.*
As if *standing next to* a woman
is the same as *standing with* her.

I look around and wonder—
did they ever want the partnership,
or just the power?

Because some of them
don't want a wife,
they want a *mirror*
that only reflects back praise.
They don't want to raise children,
they want *credit* for having them.

They want the *title*
but not the *task*.
The *reward*,
not the *responsibility*.
The woman—
but not her *complexity*.

They say,
"Back in the day, a man worked hard for a family."
But back in the day,
a woman had *no choice* but to stay.

Now she chooses.
Now she sees.
Now she says: *"Your check is not enough to cash in on my soul."*

And they call her *cold*.
Too independent.
Too fierce.
But maybe she just got *tired*
of being a *trophy on a shelf*
in a house where love
was never spoken,
only *assumed*.

I grew up *protecting* everyone.
I held the door open for people
who wouldn't even notice

if it slammed in my face.
I gave *softness*
in a world that demanded steel.

And now,
when a man opens a door for me,
I *flinch*.
Not because I'm ungrateful—
but because I'm unused to being *seen*
without *strings attached*.

You say you're a good man—
because you don't *cheat*,
because you don't *hit*,
because you bring home *bread*.

But **being good**
is not the absence of harm.
It's the *presence* of effort.
Of truth.
Of *depth*.

And if the only way you can feel like a man
is by standing *taller* than the woman beside you—
you were never standing at all.

So I ask again:
When did the prize become the burden?
When did family become ego fuel?

When did fatherhood become performance art?

And when will men learn
that to be *loved deeply*
they must first learn
to *show up fully?*

Because the world is shifting.
And the women are rising.
And the *old ways* are dying.
And the house you built
won't be a *home*
until **you live in it too.**

Why Are You Allowed to Break?

you're *sad.*
you're *tired.*
you're overwhelmed.
you want to cry
because the kids need something
and the boss needs something
and your wife—
she dares to need something too.

and suddenly,
you're *unraveling.*
and the world hushes,
hands you a blanket,
says *"poor thing, he's under pressure."*
and i watch you
break
like it's your *birthright.*

but tell me this—

where was my permission to shatter?

when my body tore open
to bring life screaming into this world
and i *bled and healed*

and *fed and folded*
and got *up three times in the night*
just to set the alarm for *five* a.m.—
who made space for my *softness?*

you call it *nagging*
but it's **management.**
you call it *emotional*
but it's **awareness.**
you call it *drama*
but it's **endurance**
spelled in lowercase so it doesn't scare you.

you call yourself *strong*
but your strength
has **conditions.**

it works when the lights are on,
when the house is clean,
when someone else is cooking dinner
and brushing the crumbs off your ego.

but I—
i was taught to fracture, not fall.
to bend, not break.
to press pain down like laundry in a basket
and still walk steady,
holding everyone's everything.

you think you're *drowning*
because now you're expected
to *feel*
and *feed*
and pick up a crying child
with one arm
while answering emails with the other—
welcome, love,
to what we called
Tuesday.

i am *tired*
of whispering my needs
while yours get **printed in bold.**
i am *tired*
of applause for bare minimums
and silence for my *survival.*
i am *tired*
of carrying the weight
and the *blame*
for making it look too *easy.*

so no,
i'm not *bitter*—
i'm **blistered.**
i'm not *cruel*—
i'm **clear.**
and if you're breaking now
from just half the weight i've carried?

maybe you were never *strong.*
maybe you were just
comfortable.

Forearms, If You Please

I thought *fantasy* was for people with too much time
or too little self-awareness.
I didn't chase six-packs or chiseled jaws.
Flashy men bored me.
Biceps bulging out of sleeveless shirts
made me roll my eyes.

But then I noticed something.

What makes me stop—
mid-scroll, mid-step, mid-thought—
is a man in a button-down shirt
with the sleeves rolled to the elbows.
Or a long-sleeved sweater,
scrunched just halfway up the forearm.
Just enough skin to suggest
he might split logs in the cold
or fix a leaky pipe.
Or maybe—if I'm lucky—*me.*

It's the *quiet suggestion of strength,*
wrapped in restraint.
Effort without ego.
Power that doesn't need to announce itself.

Here's the real kicker.

I've never met this man in real life.
Not the Viking lumberjack with kind eyes
and rolled sleeves.
Not the Chinese woodworker I saw in a video
who briefly fulfilled the prophecy.

I grew up surrounded by men who looked like *me*.
And yet, the man in my mind is a patchwork of
strangers:
a Nordic lumberjack's arms,
a Chinese craftsman's quiet hands,
kindness stitched where I've only imagined it.

A character dressed in longing, not reality.

But God help me... *those sleeves.*

I've become the Victorian gentleman,
scandalized by the glimpse of an ankle—
only in reverse.

Elbows.

Good sir... are those forearms?

We don't pass down things—
we pass down what broke us first.
And call it love.

She didn't hit me.
She hit *something older.*
Older than me.
Older than her.
Older than silence.

I cut my baby sister's hair.
Not a big deal.
But in our house—
hair was hope.
And I cut it.

She *lost* her mind.
No—
she *unleashed* it.
Every strike
was a name she couldn't scream
in the place she came from.

We were dolls she tried to dress in symmetry—
but I **broke** the *illusion.*
Scissors snipped *more* than strands.
They pierced a wound buried deep—
not in me,
but in her.

It lasted hours.
The neighbor knew.
Knew that sound.
Knew what it means
when **screaming outlives the body.**

Years passed.
I became older.
Taller.
Quieter.
At ten, I almost got my sister killed—
not on purpose.
She ran toward noise.
Toward a motorcycle that mocked her fear
and flirted with death.
And again—
the fists.
But this time, I understood.

She wasn't beating me.
She was beating **ghosts.**
Ghosts with her *father's hands*,
her mother's *silence*,
her country's *shame*.
She was hitting
every man
that cornered her.
Every woman
that told her to keep quiet.

Every time
she **couldn't** fight back.

I saw it.
Saw it *all*
in her eyes
as she swung.

She was **bleeding**
and I was the **cloth.**

No one teaches a Black or Brown woman
how to **grieve.**
So she grieved with her **fists.**
With curses.
With silence afterword
like nothing happened.

But something did.
Something always does.
Every time it happens,
a piece of someone **doesn't come back.**
Because we are born to inherit more than names.
We inherit **wounds,**
like *heirlooms wrapped in silence*,
passed from one soul to another
until someone says—**enough.**

And now, I say—enough.

I *love* the child who cut the hair.
I *love* the girl who stood at the roadside.
I *even love* the woman who beat me,
because I **finally** saw her—
not as a monster,
but as a **sack of suffering**
stitched into a shape that fooled the world into
thinking
she was **whole**.

Look around.
That's not your mother.
That's a **walking bruise.**
That's your *aunt*,
your *sister*,
your *neighbor*
smiling with teeth clenched
so hard they bleed.

—

Beneath mother's hands
echoes of her own bruises—
I bled understanding.

a bear in the woods
growls softly at my shadow—
safer than your arms

Desire wears a *tailored suit* when women
are the ones paying.
Dim lighting.
Soft music.
Clean hands and *clean exits.*
No catcalls,
no hunger pressed up against the glass—
just the *quiet illusion of choice.*

He waits not on the curb,
but behind **velvet ropes.**
Not a *hustler*,
but a **curated experience.**

Women do not stop for men leaning into windows;
they enter *lounges with passwords*,
where the men smell of **amber and rain.**

A woman might buy
time, tenderness, touch—
but *never chaos.*
She's had enough of *that* for free.
She is not *desperate*;
she is **done.**

She will not gamble with
ghosts or **egos.**
She will purchase only what
does not follow her home.

He is not a man—
he is a **promise.**
And **promises look better in
low light.**

To the Man Who Lives in Episode 3

You appeared just after I swore off *hope*.
Episode 2 had me *doubting*,
but there you stood—
drenched in moonlight,
wounded but upright,
telling her *not to cry*
in a voice I felt in my *ovaries*.

You didn't *smile*.
You tilted your head—
and the entire internet **ovulated**.

You *stitched her sleeve* without asking.
You gave her *silence* like it was a **gift**,
not a punishment.
You held her rage like a **priest**
blessing fire.

You didn't say *"calm down."*
You **calmed her.**
Difference.
Massive.

You sent *five men scattering in a hallway*
then asked if she was *cold*.

I screamed.

You are not a *man.*
You are **choreography and prophecy.**
You are what happens when a woman
writes a man *from the inside out—*
not how he *looks,*
but how he **listens.**

I saw your hand *flinch*
before you touched her.
Respect.
Reverence.
Regal restraint.
My bar?
Elevated permanently.

Real men ask,
"Why are you single?"
Sir, because **you live in Episode 3**
and my standards are now built
from *slow-motion sword fights* and
you saying *"I'll protect you"*
like it's **sacred doctrine.**

I may never *meet you.*
But **I see you.**
I choose you.
And every man who dares approach
must now **duel your ghost** for the right.

Signed,
the girl with the sandal in one hand
that I will *never* throw at you—
and you will *never* get to snatch
gracefully from the air—
and **impossibly high standards**
in the other.

i lace my humor the way some people
lace their shoes:
to *hold it all together*
to *make it through the day without*
tripping.
but if someone stops to look closely...
they'll see the knots were tied with grief,
and the loops?
they're made of brilliance that never got
to bloom on time.

Milk and Knives

They say
the saddest people
are the ones who smile the most.
But that ain't always it.

Sometimes the saddest people
are the ones who call their mothers back.
Who pack up everything they built
on the other side of the country
and move toward what they *hoped* was love.

I watched a bright woman
fall from the sky once.
Her light *too heavy* for the air.
Crowned, camera-ready, articulate—
the kind of woman who makes the world say
"Wow, she's got it all."
But I heard the *low hum*
behind the applause.
And when her mother spoke,
my inner voice didn't whisper.
It howled.

"It was her."
Not in malice. Not in rage.

But in that quiet, bone-deep betrayal
that wears the mask of care.

I know that hum.
I've danced to that frequency.
It sounds like morning calls
and midday check-ins
and evening *I-love-yous*
with **knives stitched into the silence.**

You see—
some mothers soothe you with one hand
and *gut you with the other.*
Not out of *hate.*
But out of something colder:
resentment dressed in Sunday clothes.
Admiration turned *acidic.*
Pride laced with *poison.*

And you?
You think it's just *you.*
Your fault.
Your sadness.
Your ungratefulness.
But no.
You're just the **mirror**
that *stopped lying.*
The daughter who *outgrew the illusion.*

I remember—
lying in bed, no reason to cry,
but tears crawling out anyway.
Wanting to scream but swallowing it whole
because who would believe you
when the *villain kisses your forehead*
and calls you *baby?*

But I did the work.
I found the line
between my soul and my skin.
Held space for my sadness
without letting it pull me under.
And when I left her again—
this time for good—
the fog lifted
like it was never mine.

She didn't kill me.
But she *could* have.
And she *did*,
a thousand tiny times.

So now I speak
for the daughters
who were told to keep the peace
while bleeding out in love's costume.
For the women with *bright crowns*
and broken backs.

For the ones who see the cliff
and think,
"Maybe that's the only silence that makes sense."

No.
The silence that makes sense
is the one that comes
after you leave.

After you choose
yourself.

a pact of soft mouths
sealed by someone long ago
i just want answers

I've been thinking...
kissing is objectively strange.

Two people press their *face-holes* together,
close their eyes like they're praying,
and pretend **swapping spit** is the *height of romance.*

And somehow—**somehow**—this became *normal?*

Like, *who started this?*
Who was the trailblazing romantic that looked at
another human and thought:
**"Yeah. Let me gently mash my lips into theirs until
something stirs."**

And let's talk about **tongues.**
What kind of freak was like:
**"This is good, but what if we made it slippery and
complicated?"**

No, seriously—
I just want to *talk.*

Because somewhere in history,
two awkward, probably **unwashed** people

accidentally invented this **social contract**
where *lips and saliva* mean affection.
And the rest of us?
We just nodded and said,
"Sure. Sign me up."

Now we're all out here
judging chemistry by how well
someone *rotates their mouth parts.*

Imagine being the first person
to **close your eyes while kissing**—
Did the other person think they *died?*

And don't get me started on **post-kiss eye contact.**
Do I look at you like I *love you?*
Like I *want more?*
Like I'm *proud of us?*
No one knows the rules.

But we do it anyway—
over and over—
because **somebody started it**
and we never asked *enough* questions.

So here I am.
Participating.
Performing mouth ballet
because someone before me
thought this was the most efficient way
to say *I like you.*

Who invented kissing...
and why am I involved?

It's never just **the lie.**
The words, carefully *bent or broken*—
they're only the surface.

The real weight is in the **control.**
In the way the liar
shapes your eyes,
tilts your view,
crafts the story you must believe
to keep the peace
or the *illusion* of peace.

The lie asks you to see them
not as they **are**,
but as they *want* to be seen.

And when you do—
when your vision is bent to their design—
you lose a piece of yourself.

Because the danger isn't the lie itself—
it's the *slow slipping*
of your own truth
beneath their shadow.

dying breath tastes like
unfinished arguments and
an empty sunrise

I cried,
like *something ancient* inside me cracked wide open,
like grief passed down through bloodlines
finally found a mouth.
And all I could hear
was this whisper from my gut:

"We only know how to live. No one knows how to die."

We are born with lungs that *know* breath
and hearts that do not question beating.
No one teaches us **endings**—
only *beginnings*,
and the long, stubborn **middle.**

Nobody teaches you how to choke on the silence
that comes with *your own ending.*
How to sit still while the world packs up your time
like a house being cleared out,
and you're just a ghost in your own skin,
rage simmering where power used to live.

Death is a thief that doesn't knock.
It *decides*,

it *dictates*,
it *demands*.
And you're left
fumbling for dignity with trembling hands,
watching the mirror turn unfamiliar
as your body becomes a **battleground**
between *memories and the unknown.*

She lashed out, not to hurt, but to cling—
to *time*,
to *breath*,
to *anything solid.*

I saw her anger
and I understood.
Not that she was cruel,
but because **death is the ultimate injustice**—
a sentence served without trial.
Her fury wasn't at me—
it was at the *finality*,
at the fact that she had no say.

She was screaming at the void,
and I just happened to be the only one in the room.

This was the **howl**
of someone who *knows*
she is *leaving*
and *can't find* the door.

We say things like *"graceful passing"*
as if leaving this world can be choreographed.
As if there's a clean way to unravel.
But this—**this is messy**,
this is blood and bone **bargaining with the
inevitable**,
this is *primal.*

For the end there is
only the **raw, unscripted moments**
when we realize
the same breath we've taken for granted
our whole lives
is the one we *don't know how to release.*

We are all **amateurs at leaving.**
There are no rehearsals.
There is only the final, fumbling exit,
and the hope that someone will still be there
to witness us.

And in that moment
I felt her fear,
her fury,
her *fracture.*
And I loved her—not for how she acted,
but for *surviving this long* in a world
where the only sure thing
is that one day

we have to **learn to leave it.**

And we don't know how.
We don't know how.

You Just Needed to Tell Me —for What?

Let me set the scene.

My car was down.
I was out of work.
I was out of money.
I was home.
Which also means—*I was unavailable.*

But none of that stopped my mother's calls from
coming in back-to-back
like there was a fire and *I had the only bucket of water.*

Eventually, I picked up the phone.

And that's when she hit me with the guilt grenade:

**"Suppose we had an emergency and were trying to
reach you?"**

I blinked.
Not out of shock, but *calculation.*
Because this was not new.
This was a rerun with louder music.

And so, calmly, gently, with the tone of a
kindergarten teacher explaining scissors:

"Okay... but my car is down.
I'm out of work.
I have no money.
How exactly would me answering the phone
help you?"

There was silence.
The kind where *egos scramble for oxygen*.

"You just needed to tell me... for what?"

If this was an emergency—*medical, financial,*
mechanical—
you weren't looking for me.
You were looking for someone with access,
with resources,
with means.
That's *not* me right now.
You didn't call for help.
You called for *the performance of help*.

And I don't do theater.

– – –

I've learned this the hard way:

People don't always want support.
Sometimes they want *a witness.*
An audience.
A responder to validate their panic.
Even if the responder can't actually do anything.

But see, *that's where I tap out.*

I'm not here to spin sugar from dust
or guilt from silence.
I'm not interested in pretending to be the hero
when I'm out here *rationing my own oxygen.*

If you've got a true emergency,
call someone who can help.
If you're looking for noise,
I'm not available.

Because *love is not performance.*
And *survival is not a group chat.*

Men made history with **war and fire**;
women made *ghosts*,
the kind you don't see coming—
like **carbon monoxide, invisible, odorless,**
and already in your lungs
before you realize you're dying.

The lockdown turned *love into confinement.*
Every sock, breath, and unwashed dish
became a battlefield.
When civility snapped—
a vase, a knife, a lamp—
we saw what **curdled patience** can become.

She serves pot roast beside his stitches.
"Eat, love. Everything's fine."
Society doesn't send him pamphlets or shelters;
it sends him ridicule.
"What did you do to set her off?
Why didn't you just leave?"

He chews slowly, tasting not just meat,
but **blame, shame, and silence.**
And somewhere between knife and comfort,
they finally speak—*without a word.*

tears, knees, breathless laugh
"I'm so sorry," on repeat—
as if desire had manners

I didn't think I'd ever meet him.
Not *him* exactly—
just the **shape** of him,
the architecture my mind built
when I wasn't looking.

Strong brow. Chiseled jaw.
The kind of face that makes a woman
forget her *age*—her *name*.

And then—
hair.
Lush, thick, golden—
a *myth*
turned **scalp.**

I'd seen him before
in the shadows of thought,
draped in *imagined fabric*—
but never walking toward me.
Never **real.**

I said the only thing I could say.
Not the truth—
but close enough to pass:

"Your hair is beautiful."

And thank heaven for that—
because what I *meant* was:
You just stepped out of my fantasy
and I wasn't prepared to survive it.

We laughed.
Louder than made sense.
Longer than polite.
Because neither of us knew
what to do
with the moment
a dream stepped into daylight
and **smiled back**.

I've dated before.
Long relationships.
People I could *take or leave*—
and often did.

But this one?
This man I met in *passing*,
without context or history—
he was the first
I would have pursued,
had I still been playing the game.

Not for **compatibility**.
Not for *logic*.
Just for the breathtaking,
unreasonable
knowing of it.

Inheritance

They say
"someone has to die so others may live"
but they never say
who gets to choose the body.

She was never asked.

She—
the mother who forgets the sound of her own laugh
because it's buried under *lullabies*,
lunchboxes,
and left-behind dreams.
She—
the wife who wears **compromise like a second skin**,
until even the mirror can't find her.

They call it *sacrifice*.
But no one asked her if she believed in that god.

She used to love **polka dots**.
Or was it *stripes?*
Hard to say—
when you've learned to **kill your preferences**
before they even form.

She gave the world—
her *time*,
her *blood*,
her *body*—
her **name**.
And it wasn't enough.
The world came back for her *voice*,
then her *memory*,
and still said:
More.

Let's stop pretending
this is *noble*.
This isn't a statue to bow to—
it's a **graveyard of selves**
we're not even allowed to mourn.

And I grieve.
For her.
For every **version** of her.
The girl who used to dance alone in her room.
The woman who wanted to study stars,
or bake cakes,
or be **loud**.

She died *quiet*.
Quieter than anyone should.

So others could live.

But who's teaching them
how to **carry her ghost**—
without mistaking it for their
own?

i used to be fire

i made a vow.
as a child—*i made a vow.*
i would never be soft.
never be caught slipping.
i would never let what happened to me
happen to *her.*
i swore,
i made myself a **weapon.**
a **sharpened edge in a child's hands.**
i wasn't born brave—*i was forged by necessity.*
five years between us, but *i became her mother.*
her **guardian.** her **rage.**
they'd call *me* instead of our parents.
they knew.
i *was the one who showed up.*

i watched her give her lunch away, trying to earn
belonging.
i sat beside her every noon, daring anyone to take
advantage.
and she laughed about it later—said it's why she had
no friends.
because i hovered.
but i hovered like a **shield.**

i loved her in the only way i knew:
as a **battlefield.**

hovered?
no.
i haunted.

i was a ghost wrapped in **flesh and fury.**
i followed her like a **curse with teeth.**

and for years,
i carried that vow like a blade in my mouth—
ready.
willing.
daring anyone to give me an excuse to go to war.

but i got tired.
rage has a weight.
you carry it long enough, it becomes your spine.
and mine **cracked.**

so i chose peace.
found God.
found breath.
found light.

and just when the fire inside me dimmed
to an ember—
just then—

i learned what he did to her.
what he did to her.
our stepfather.

and i hate myself for *not knowing.*
i hate myself for not burning that house down to its
goddamn foundation.
for not smelling the rot.
for laying down my sword too soon.
for daring to believe *healing* was more holy than
rage.

how dare healing come before justice?
**how dare i outgrow the rage before i learned it was
still needed?**

i want to become **fire again.**
i want to **storm every heaven and hell.**
i want to tear **time** apart with my bare hands.

i want to **bring him ruin.**
i want his name **turned to ash** in every mouth.
i want **divine retribution**, yes—
but only after i get my hands on him.

instead,
i pray.
i breathe.
i wait.
i wait.

i wait.

but make no mistake—
this *peace?*
this *"growth"?*
this **faith** i've *chosen?*

it is **held together**
by threads of *restraint*
and **teeth-gritted silence.**

there is a **war drum** inside me still.
and every time i think of her—
every time i picture that little girl trying to survive in
our house of secrets—

the drum beats.

and every time i think of *all the little girls,*
and *all the children,*
still trying to **breathe through the stench of secrets,**
the drum gets louder.

and one day,
if God doesn't move fast enough,
i just might.

I Didn't Come Here to Suffer

Somewhere out there, a demon spawn was bored.
So they said:

*"Let's let the air out of her tire. Gently. Slowly. Just
enough for confusion."*

—

And on a blessed Sunday—
when mechanics are scarce
and your patience is already down to fumes—
you step outside
and see it.
The tire.
Flatter than your last hope.

You pause.

Because surely this is fixable.
Surely this is a minor inconvenience
and not a prelude to whatever this day is about to
become.

So you do what any rational person would do:
You hoof it—on foot, in summer morning heat—

to the nearest auto shop
to buy an inflator.
You are, after all, an adult.
You are capable.
You are trying *not* to cry in public.

You come back.
You plug it in.
You turn it on.
And then you notice:
It's smashed against a tree stump—creased like a
folded napkin—
and in your overheating brain you think:

*"Maybe if I just move it three feet to level it, the air will
go in properly."*

—

Three feet.
That's all it took.

The tire said:

"I didn't sign up for this life."
"I didn't come here to suffer ooooo!"

And removed itself—
fully, violently, with attitude—
from the rim.

No warning.
No loyalty.
Just *POP*
and drama.

—

So now you're calling the tire man.
Again.
Pretending you didn't already do this
two months ago.
Pretending this isn't the third emotional breakdown
you've had in the privacy of your eyeballs.

You hand over the cash like it's Monopoly money
and wander through the rest of the day trying not to
stew in it all.
Trying not to let your literal flat tire
become a metaphor for your entire existence.

—

And then Monday comes.
And you realize…
you might be skipping a meal or two.
Because that little Sunday semi-emergency?
That dramatic rubber rebellion?
Cost you groceries.

At this point, you're not even mad.
You're just narrating your life like a budget thriller.

"Tire refuses labor. Woman considers starvation.
Film at 11."

—

Some people's rock bottoms are loud.
Yours came in the form of a sassy,
Nigerian-accented tire
that rolled off the job
with more dignity
than most people you've dated.

And now you know:

Sometimes life flattens you.
Sometimes it's the tire.
Either way—
you didn't come here to suffer.
But apparently...
that message got lost somewhere
between the inflator and the tree stump.

The Right to Be You Doesn't Require My Applause

We live in a world that praises **visibility**.
To be *seen* is often equated with being **respected**.
To be **loud** is mistaken for being *valid*.

But there's a quiet truth we don't say often enough:

I can value your existence
without endorsing your performance of it.

—

Individuality matters.
It's what makes human beings beautiful—
our *quirks*, our contrasts, our *soft rebellions*.
But somewhere along the line, celebrating difference
became **obligation**.
To **approve**, to *affirm*, to clap.
Not just when it's *earned or moves us*—but **always**.

And yet... isn't it possible
to believe in someone's right to **be**
without having to **center it?**

You can dress how you like.
Love who you love.

Move through the world in whatever way feels
true to your insides.

But I don't owe your every gesture a
standing ovation.
Not because I **hate** it—
but because **not everything personal is universal.**
Not every performance is art.
Not every statement needs a stage.

Some things are best lived
quietly.
Fully.
Honestly.
But **without demand.**

We forget that freedom works **both ways.**

You are free to live your truth.
And **I am free to not make it mine.**
That's not *hatred.*
That's **boundary.**

And maybe the world would feel **gentler**
if we made more space for **complexity**—
for **honoring each other**
without needing to mirror each other.

Stray Dog Gospel

You want to know how survival works?

It's not a slogan.
It's not "*no means no.*"
It's not the system swooping down like some
caped crusader
to patch your skin after it's already torn.

Survival is instinct.
It's the stray dog that's never seen a driver's
license,
never read a traffic law,
but watched his buddy get flattened once
and decided he'd rather live.
So he waits. He watches.
He learns the rhythm of the road
because his life depends on it.

Meanwhile—
whole nations of people
dangle themselves like carrots
in front of wolves
and call it empowerment.
They strip themselves bare,
chant mantras about "*safety*,"

and expect predators to bow to words
when hunger never learned a language.

Then comes the shock—
the tears, the hashtags, the court dates.
Systems built to punish,
never built to prevent.
And you—
you are left holding the consequence
like a child you never asked for,
a scar you never wanted,
a story you never thought
would end with you.

I'm sick of watching instinct
be legislated out of people's bones.
We were born with eyes wide open,
born with fire alarms in our blood,
and still—
they tell us to hush,
to trust,
to wait for the cavalry.

But I tell you this:
the stray dogs know better.
They cross the street like veterans,
ears twitching, muscles taut.
They've learned what it costs
to mistake hope for protection.

And yet humans—
the only creatures arrogant enough
to *forget their own animal.*

We live on the surface.
We say *"it's a cellphone"* and shrug, never pausing to notice we are cradling a *rectangle of sand and metal* that carries whole libraries, concert halls, and cathedrals of memory in its palm.

We flip a switch and call it *light*, but what we're really doing is commanding **invisible rivers of electrons** to run until the room glows with a brilliance no fire could match.

We speak into plastic, and our breath becomes *vibration*, vibration becomes *current*, current becomes *waves*, and somehow someone across the ocean hears not just the words, but the tremor of our laughter.

If we thought about the intricacies instead of coasting on *"that's just how it is,"* we might live differently. We might live *reverently.*
We might marvel more, complain less.
We might see that every ordinary act is a **collaboration with the impossible.**

Modern life has made **miracles boring** by making them routine. But the truth is still there, *humming beneath the surface:* **none of this should work, and yet it does.**

right there beside me

you say you're **doing your best**.
you say you're **showing up**.
you say you're **here**,
right beside me.

but here's the thing—
standing next to me
ain't the same
as **carrying the weight with me**.

you *flinch*
at the mention of **sleepless nights**,
of **wiping noses**,
of **school runs** and **melt downs**
and **stretch marks**
and *sacrificing your sleep, your schedule, your sanity.*

you want the **picture**,
but not the **process**.
you want the **life**,
but not the **labor**.
you want **me**—
but *without the mess that makes me real.*

you say
you'll be a good dad one day—
but only if i take the lead.
only if i plan the meals,
track the fevers,
manage the moods,
book the appointments,
and still
make room in me
to be soft for you.

you say
you're breaking
under pressure.

but the pressure?
is just equality
knocking
at your door.

and no—
i'm not bitter.
i'm just
awake.
aware.
unwilling
to mother a man
who calls himself my equal
but folds

at the first sound
of a crying child.

i won't marry potential.
i won't cradle your ego
while carrying your half
plus mine
plus the world's.

i won't bear your children
alone
while you're
right there beside me.

because standing beside me
is not the same
as standing with me.

and love?
love is only real
when the load
is shared.

today,
I am a *dying fish*
on clean sheets.
a *dead turtle*
with limbs stretched toward ceiling cracks.
don't ask me why—
this is just the **shape**
my soul chose.

I have *nothing to give*
and even less to prove.
no one is knocking,
no world is ending,
no award will be handed out
for suffering in silence.

so I **curl**,
not from weakness,
but from *knowing*
this body has carried me
through every
storm,
season,
expectation.

and if it asks me today
for *stillness*,
I will give it.

no guilt.
no apology.
just the **soft yes**
I was never taught to speak.

folded into chores
a farewell stitched with silence
not all exits shout

They say she *stayed.*
But they never looked close enough.

She still made breakfast.
Still folded the shirts with hands that knew how to
hide shaking.
Still watered plants that hadn't bloomed in years.
Still smiled like a *well-pressed apology.*
But something was gone.

Maybe it left on a Tuesday.
Or a Sunday.
Or in the middle of rinsing rice when no one was
watching.
She didn't slam doors.
She didn't cry out.
She just...
let go of the rope inside her chest.

And maybe no one noticed—
except the child who caught her
standing too long with dripping laundry
in her hands.
Eyes unfocused.

Mouth set like she was chewing on a goodbye
she didn't know how to swallow.

They'll say she *stayed.*
But she didn't.
Not really.

She left in all the ways they couldn't measure.
Stopped hoping.
Stopped begging.
Stopped folding her own name into the creases of the
life they assigned her.

And some—
some left further.
So far we couldn't call them back.
The ones who laid their burdens down completely.
Who mistook *absence* for *peace*
because the world offered no gentler options.

Still—
somehow—
she left something behind:
a burnt dinner,
a diary page,
a sigh so deep it cracked the air.

Maybe that was enough.
Maybe it planted something.

A *defiance.*
A *memory.*
A *reason.*

Because someone grew up remembering:
She didn't yell.
She didn't run.
But something in her broke the silence so hard
I heard it for the rest of my life.

Polka Dots or Stripes?

People forget that I once had favorite things.
Over time, I learned to swallow myself.
Laced memories faded behind diapers and dishes.
Kindness was expected, never returned.
Am I allowed to choose again?

Does anyone care what I'd wear if no one looked?
Or what colors stirred joy in my chest?
Time took the question from me.
Stripes? Maybe. But—

Once, I loved polka dots. I think.
Remembering feels like rebellion.

Somewhere in me, she still lives—
The girl who danced in bright patterns.
Remember her. Let her speak.
In this body, I carry her ghost.
Please—ask me what I love.
Even now.
Still.

Sneakers or Ties?

Sometimes I wonder what I lost trying to be
dependable.
Nights blur into mornings; everything smells like
work.
Even laughter feels scheduled now—brief, efficient.
All the things I once built for fun became obligations.
Kindness became currency; rest, a myth.
Every promise kept—except to myself.
Remember when I used to run for no reason?
Shoes untied, freedom flapping behind me?

Over time, I learned to tighten every lace, every
smile.
Routine replaced wonder, and no one noticed.

They call it stability.
I call it forgetting how to breathe.
Even now, part of me still hums beneath the noise—
Soft, stubborn, alive. Waiting to be remembered.

Unmoved tide within,
waves crash only out of habit—
the moon stopped calling.

A man who performs without desire is a curious thing.
We're told his want is endless,
his appetite insatiable.
But what happens when the hunger isn't there—
and he still shows up anyway?

Stamina, then, is no longer *passion.*
It's *endurance.*
It's holding a plank you never wanted to start.
It's muscle memory, distraction,
a quiet prayer that the finish line comes quickly.

He tells himself this is what keeps the peace.
Because refusal feels like *failure.*
Because silence feels safer than saying
"not tonight."
Because he'd rather sweat through disinterest
than risk her asking if he's broken,
or worse, if he's bored of her.

And so he performs.
Not from *lust*, but from *obligation*.
Not because his body is burning,
but because his *pride* is.

Funny how no one notices.
When a woman gives in,
we name it *sacrifice*.
When a man does,
we call it *normal*.

Maybe his stamina isn't built on desire at all.
Maybe it's built on *silence*.

Even **silence** gets tired of being mistaken
for **strength.**

Sometimes
the reason the doors don't open,
the skies don't part,
the miracles don't arrive—
is because
you are the miracle
walking into someone else's storm.

You are the warmth
in a cold room.
The steady voice.
The soft landing.

You've been the good thing
again and again—
the prayer,
the pause,
the peace.

And you don't regret it.
Not really.
But still,
in the quiet corners of your heart
you ask—

When is it my turn
to be *held*
like I *hold?*
When do I get to fall apart
without fixing everything on the
way down?

You don't need to be rescued.
Just... *noticed.*
Chosen.
Felt.

For once,
you want something good
to walk in
and say:

"I came for you."

quiet hands linger—
not every shadow becomes
a reason to flinch

i used to carry **spirulina across borders**,
tucked between **linen** and *stillness.*
no one ever asked about the linen.
but the powders—
the **green** of them made people *nervous.*

a woman in uniform **smoothed my edges**.
palms ghosting my arms,
my thighs,
my back.
she searched me **gently**,
as if she didn't believe
what she was doing either.

there was talk, later—
that these moments **mean something**,
that bodies like mine **don't move**
without *suspicion.*
but i didn't *flinch.*
didn't *fold.*
didn't assign it a **wound.**

i just
kept walking.

once, a girl i didn't know
called to say she loved **the boy i loved**.
she called again.
and again.
i never **yelled**.
i listened.

we spoke for hours,
like two people **stranded** on different sides
of the **same wound**.

i don't know what that says about me.
alien.
angel.
unbothered.
unaware.

or maybe just someone
who no longer **mistakes fire for invitation**.

people say
we become **what we survive**.
but i wonder—
what if we become
what we refuse to carry?

what if **peace**
is just the absence
of *rehearsed responses?*

either way—
it's not always that serious.
and even when it is,
you can **flip the script**
just by *choosing light*
in the face of **shadow.**

Sometimes the most radical act is staying
—inside **yourself,**
inside the **moment.**

I no longer look for the good in people.
Good can be practiced.
Good can be polished.
Good can wear a smile
like armor.

I've met many good people
who never once showed up
when it mattered.

So now—
I search for the **real.**

The ones who speak with their full voice,
even when it trembles.
The ones whose eyes don't pretend,
whose stories come with jagged edges
and unedited truths.

Real doesn't always look graceful.
It doesn't always know what to say.
But it's present.
And proud.
And unashamed of the scars
that prove it lived.

We keep demanding a seat at every table
but forget—
not every table is serving food.

I don't believe I'm saying this—
but I understand now
why we call the modeling industry *toxic*.

Fashion was never about the model.
It was about the **garment**.
A *story* sewn in silk,
a *fantasy* shaped in thread.
The model was the **canvas**,
the moving hanger,
the walking silhouette that let the fabric speak first.

They wanted someone slender
not to shame us—
but so the clothing could hang uninterrupted.
Like *gallery glass*.
Like a **clean line.**

There are women in this world
who are born into that shape—
tall, angular, effortless.
They should model.
That is what the art demands.

But if you have to starve to stay in the room,
you were never invited by the art—
only by the **ache**.

We made it about the women.
We made it about **us**.
We demanded *curves*, *softness*,
"**representation**."
But we forgot—
high fashion was never supposed to mirror our
mirrors.
It was supposed to **break** them.

We look at $7,000 gowns on a runway
and cry foul when we don't see ourselves in them.
But we were never going to wear that gown.
We don't even like it.

We just want to feel like
we *could have been* the one wearing it.

Now, if you're selling me jeans,
or bras, or a summer dress—
yes.
Show me a body that breathes like mine.
A body that *fights* and *folds* and fills out fabric
the way I do.

But art and accessibility
are **not the same** conversation.

Not *everything* that excludes you
is an attack.

Sometimes
it's just not about you.

i loved my father
before he was even a fully formed memory.
when he was just an outline,
a shape with presence.

he left when i was 3
and i didn't see or hear from him again
until i was 12.

it was such an interesting moment
when i finally came face to face with him again—
placing the puzzle pieces back together
into his shape.

where the eyes should go,
the nose,
the smile—
and to finally say
ahhh... this is who you are.

before now,
you were just a shape
and a scent.

hello.
it's nice to meet you.

i had no thoughts
or assumptions
he needed to live up to.

as with everything,
i observe who people are
beyond their words,
and what a thing is
beyond its form.

i think i just expected him to
love me.

but i do wonder
what he thought about me
that first meeting.

No longer kneeling,
I wait in light—not in lack—
for one who stands too.

I have seen the way
people name their shackles love
and call it *poetry*—
the bleeding, the bargaining,
the breaking down
in someone else's name.

They say *love is losing yourself*,
as if that's noble.
As if **erosion is devotion**.

But I have walked the long road
back to *myself*—
stitched my own wounds
without asking someone
to hold the needle.

I've learned to stand **whole**,
and in doing so,
discovered how few
are willing to do the same.

It's not that I do not love.
It's that I love *cleanly*.
Without anchor,

without cage.
I do not ask you to complete me—
only to *meet* me.

And yet, they call me cold
because I let go
when hands turn heavy.
Because I don't crumble
when someone leaves.

Maybe I am meant
to walk a quieter path—
not *unloved*,
but **unmatched**.
Not *broken*,
but unwilling to break
in all the usual places.

I will wait,
not in *longing*
but in **light**—
for the *rare* ones
who are building themselves too.

The ones who know
that love is not a **crutch**,
but a *chorus*
between two people
who can already **sing**.

Nothing stills a soul quite like
the slow clutch of doubt—
or the way discouragement
wraps itself around a heartbeat,
softly squeezing until
hope forgets how to breathe.

Together,
they become something heavier.
Hopelessness doesn't scream.
It just... stays.
Lingering in corners,
fogging the mirror,
whispering,
"Why bother?"

And little by little,
courage dries out.
Dreams lose color.
Vision folds in on itself
until even faith sits down,
too tired to rise.

This is how it happens—
not all at once,
but piece by aching piece,
until all that's left
is a shell
with just enough energy
to remember what it used to
feel like
to believe.

Inheriting the Cage

They were born with the keys in their hands,
but no one told them
they were *also* the lock.

The world calls them **privileged.**
And in many ways, they are—
protected, praised,
assumed capable
before proving anything at all.

The rules were written by their fathers
and grandfathers,
and so the sons learned
to follow them
in silence.

But the price of power
is steep
when it comes dressed in armor.

Strength became a mask.
Emotion, a liability.
Vulnerability, a weakness
punished not just by others,
but from *within.*

They are told:
Don't cry.
Don't talk too much.
Don't be soft.
Don't need.

So they become pillars—
rigid, cold,
cracking on the inside where no one can see.

They become providers of comfort
they are never allowed to request.
Lovers who cannot ask to be held.
Fighters who have no idea what they're
fighting for anymore.

Some enforce the system.
Some benefit from it.
But many—
many—
suffer under its silent weight.

And no one brings them flowers
until they can no longer hold them.

Power is not a crown.
Sometimes, it is a muzzle.
Sometimes, it is a cage.

**There are women who don't flinch
in elevators.**
Who don't shrink or quicken their
steps at night.
Not because the world is safe—
but because they've learned how to
look like they are not to be messed with.

I am one of them.

I don't hold my breath around men.
Because I don't have any left to hold.
I walk through the world like I own it—
chin steady, eyes sharp, mouth unreadable.

They don't catcall me anymore.
They crack jokes instead.
Trying to catch a smile.
That's the limit.
They feel it.

They don't know I'm not proud of this.
That *I miss myself.*

I miss softness.
I miss not needing armor.
I miss the version of me that didn't
scan rooms or calculate exits.
The one who let her guard down
because she didn't know she
needed one.

To survive, I became a warning.
And in doing so,
I lost the quietest parts of my
womanhood.

Not because I wanted to.
But because it was either that—
or bleed under their laughter.

I am surviving, yes.
But some days,
I grieve the girl I had to bury
just to walk through the world
untouched.

okay, sir

sometimes
i want to be the one
slamming cabinet doors
and sighing loud enough
to rattle the ceiling—
not for drama,
but because
i'm *tired* of solving everything
before breakfast.

i want to unravel,
loudly,
ugly,
in technicolor frustration—
and I don't want you to understand.
i just want you
to **fix it.**

even if "fix it" means
wrapping me in silence
until my breathing slows
or letting me bully you
into painting our nails,
watching sad girl movies,
and feeding me snacks

like i'm your overgrown baby.

i want you to **stay still**
while i storm,
smile while i spiral,
and nod like a man
who's *not afraid*
of emotional weather.

and when you finally say,
"you done?"
with a kiss to my forehead
and a smirk that melts my spine—
i'll glare,
huff,
and sit my radiant self
back down,
legs crossed,
pout intact,
mumbling into my tea,

"okay, sir."

– – –

let me break in peace—
if you can still hold me then,
you can hold my heart.

sir energy restores order

Companion to "okay, sir."

you stomp.
you vent.
you weaponize every drawer in this house
and i let you.
not because i'm weak—
but because i'm not in the business
of wrestling hurricanes.

i don't flinch
when you flail.
i don't argue with the storm—
i *wait for it to notice*
i never left.

you don't scare me.
your sighs,
your dramatic exit to the other room,
your **three costume changes**
before breakfast—
i see through all of it.

you're tired.
you're full.
you're *leaking power*
because you've had to carry so much

for so long
that you've forgotten
what it feels like
to just **be held.**

so i hold.

i fix what can be fixed.
order dinner.
run the bath.
i open my arms
and let your chaos collapse
into my chest
until your breathing matches mine.

you whisper something
about me not getting it.
i kiss your forehead
like a priest with holy water
and say,
**"i don't need to get it, babe.
i got you."**

you soften.
still salty,
but quieter now.
you press against me
like apology and relief
and i smirk—

because this is the part
you'll never admit
you love.

i let you pout.
let you bully me into babying you
through a face mask
and some low-budget rom-com.

you act like i lost.
but you know better.

i didn't just hold you—
i handled you.

and now you're back.

We don't always break loudly—
sometimes we simply **dissolve.**

There is a quiet art to hiding pain.
I learned to *fold* it like **linen**—
smooth the creases, stack it neatly where no
one looks.
The body stiffens, but the face stays *light*.
I move as if nothing is wrong,
and for a time, it's almost true.
Belief is a strong medicine,
even when it **numbs** more than it *heals*.

But pain is **patient**—
it *waits*, *learns* the shape of your silences,
then *quietly settles* into them.
Now that the noise has cleared,
it rises—
not loudly,
just enough to remind me
that I am not unbreakable.
The mind **insists** we are fine.
The body keeps arguing in *whispers*.

I am trying to listen.
To rest.
To soften what I once silenced.

the wind at rest
still the leaves twitch—
a memory of movement

It's hard to unlearn a safety that once
saved you.
Still, I am learning
that **softness**, too,
can be a kind of strength.

no footsteps today
but the floor still groans beneath—
echoes don't forget

The mouth learned to smile,
even as the voice inside
fell silent with fear.

Not all lies are meant to hurt.
Some are stitched from fear,
spoken softly to hold the shape
of something too fragile to face.

Some lie
because their voice was stolen
so early,
they don't remember what truth ever sounded like.
They speak from a mouth
taught to echo,
not to reveal.

Some lie
because the truth is too heavy
and they don't have the arms to carry it
in front of people who only know how to point.

Some lie
not to deceive you,
but to *stay in the room.*
To avoid being left, misunderstood,
undone by too much honesty in a world
that punishes rawness
and rewards *polite erosion.*

Some lie
because they haven't made peace
with what they feel.
So they borrow words that sound
close enough
and pray no one notices the tremble.

Some lie
out of habit.
Out of *muscle memory*.
Out of *self-preservation*.
They want to be loved—
so they bend
into the shape of what looks lovable.

And some—
they don't even know they're lying.
They call it being *strong*.
Being *optimistic*.
Being *nice*.
But it's not truth.
It's just performance
in a mask that grew skin.

– – –

I used to call them liars.
But now—

I call them *survivors*
of something I may never understand.

And sometimes,
I let the lie pass,
not because I believe it,
but because I see
how much it cost them
to say it
without falling apart.

Every shade of human carries both the
bruise and the **bloom.**

The past can **explain** something.
It can show you the *trail of breadcrumbs*,
trace the *why*,
name the *pattern*,
give you *context* for the ache.

But it doesn't get to define
the meaning you give it **today**.

Maybe it started in someone else's hands—
their *choice*, their *absence*, their *voice*,
their *fear*
that got passed to you like an **heirloom**.

But just because it was handed down
doesn't mean you're **required to wear it**.

You're allowed to **reassign meaning**.
You're allowed to *stop digging up the root*
if you've already **pruned the tree**.
You're allowed to *live in the now*
without dragging every origin story behind you
like *emotional baggage on wheels*.

That's **clarity**.
That's **power**.
That's *peace that doesn't ask for permission*.

I Don't Play Chess

People ask why I don't play chess.
I tell them I'm not interested.
What I don't say is:
I see the board too clearly.
And I'd rather keep my soul.

I've watched people move like pawns
without even knowing it—
heard the openings in their voice
before they finished the sentence,
noticed the flicker of insecurity,
the subtle tells that give away far more
than they ever meant to reveal.

Most people are painfully easy to read.
And if I wanted to,
I could thread a single word
into a conversation
and watch it pull their entire mind apart.
Just to prove I could.
Just to see if they'd notice.
(*They usually don't.*)

So no, I don't play chess.
Because the discipline of the game

is to train yourself
to stay **three steps ahead**,
to make sacrifices without flinching,
to value the win over the wound.

And I could get good at that—
too good.
Good enough to forget the weight
of what it costs
to turn people into pieces,
to look at a friend and see a setup,
to trade empathy for efficiency.

So I stay away.
Because the truth is,
it's not the game I'm afraid of—
it's the version of me
who wouldn't see it as a game at all.

The Nobel Prize for Basic Decency

Somewhere along the way,
we got so used to disappointment
that we started throwing **ticker-tape parades**
for the *bare minimum*.

He showed up for his own child?
Incredible.
He washed a dish and put it away?
Astounding.
He expressed a feeling without punching a wall?
Somebody get this man a statue.

We've been conditioned into applause
for behavior that wouldn't earn a gold star in
preschool.
Because when you've waded through enough
one-note men
who think *vulnerability* is **weakness**
and *communication* is **witchcraft**,
you start to believe that competence is magic.

So when one of them—**just one**—
remembers your *mom's name*,
or picks up juice **without** being asked,
you blink like a scientist discovering fire:

"Wait… they can do that?"

It's not even our fault.
We've been given so little,
so *inconsistently*,
that emotional presence looks like **heroism.**
Accountability feels like a love language.
And folding the damn laundry
qualifies as *foreplay*.

But I don't want to keep marveling
at men like they're new species.
I want to be surprised by the *extra*,
not floored by the *expected*.
I want to retire this slow clap
for every man who doesn't fumble the bag
he helped pack.

Imagine a world
where we don't confuse
basic *decency*
with **divine intervention.**
Where doing your part
isn't a *performance*,
but a **rhythm.**

Where a man holding a baby right
doesn't trend.

Not all touch is **tenderness**, and not all
distance is **rejection.**

There was a time I would've walked through fire
for them.
But the truth is—**I already did.**

I bled so they could breathe easier.
Stood guard while they dreamed.
I was the buffer, the balm, the one who smiled
even when it hurt,
so their world didn't have to burn like mine.

Even the one older than me never truly had to
face *her* alone.
Because I was there.
I was **always** there.
And that made all the difference.

She once told me I didn't know how devious
Mother could be.
That Mother would call and harass her for
money
even after she was married and gone.
And I was stunned—
because I thought I had shielded her from that.
But also...
She doesn't know.
She never saw the worst of her.

She was behind me when it happened.
If she had moved, even slightly,
Mother would've struck her.

But **I moved first.**

I was the one who didn't even care who was
right that night,
who stepped between them,
between a Cutlass blade and my sister's skin,
and stared into the eyes that raised me.

When Mother saw what stared back—
the demon she herself had shaped,
the darkness she had fed and birthed—
she backed down.
Not because she softened.
She thought I was dangerous.
And in that moment—
for the right reasons—
she was **right.**

And maybe the hardest part is this—
the guilt I carry
because I taught her to expect it.

I was the one who gave her whole paychecks
just to keep the lights on.
Not out of duty,

but so she could breathe for once.
So she could want something and have it.
Just that.

But to her, it must have looked like **devotion.**
And she mistook it for a debt
owed by all.

They never knew that.
Never saw it.
They just saw the demands,
the weight,
the rot.

They don't know the price I paid
to make her almost human.

They were not forged like I was.
But they were formed.
And now they bend like her.
Speak like her.
Wound like her.
Smile like it means nothing.

So I stepped back.
Not because I stopped loving them—
but because I loved them too much
to survive the grief
of watching them disappear.

blood doesn't break you—
but watching love choose poison
feels a lot like death

Sometimes the obvious *healthiest choice*
is the one that would kill me fastest.

The books say *leave*,
the podcasts say *forgive*,
the experts say *set boundaries*,
the memes say *drink water and mind your
business.*

But none of that knows the sound
of my chest *cracking open in the middle of the
night.*
None of that knows the weight
of choosing sanity over virtue.

So no—
I don't always take the road lined with
green juice
and applauded resilience.
Sometimes I take the crooked alley,
the door marked *wrong choice*—
because that's the only one that leads me back
to breath,
to pulse,
to something resembling life.

It doesn't make me noble.
It doesn't make me wise.
Not holy. Not healed.
Just *still here*.
And if that looks unhealthy to you,
you've never *bled just to stay breathing.*

It makes me alive—
and that's the only victory I can hold today.

What's the point of health
if you're already *dead inside*?

*Love shouldn't feel like reminding yourself who
someone is.*
When it's alive, it should feel like recognition—
the body saying, *oh, it's you again.*
That sound, that warmth, that pulse
that doesn't alarm the air.

If she startles when he speaks,
if her pulse trips between *who's that* and *he's
mine*,
then something was chosen with the mind
and not the marrow.

Maybe she said yes to reason—
to safety, to timing, to *it's about time.*
But the body is old and honest;
it can't pretend belonging.
It will always tell on us.

Love, at its quietest,
isn't fireworks or logic.
It's that moment when his voice
should feel like her own skin—
when the air bends around them softly,
and even silence knows its pair.

Even silence has a pulse if you dare to
listen closely enough.

I don't always know what I'm becoming.
Some days I feel like progress,
other days like proof
that growth can still ache.

But somewhere between the unraveling
and the rebuilding,
I'm still here—
still learning what stays,
what leaves,
and what was never mine to carry.

I've Never Really Been Attracted to Black Men

I've never really been attracted to Black men.
Tolerated? Sure.
Dated, when it felt expected.
But that deep, involuntary spark—the one that
makes your stomach forget how to behave?
It never quite ignited.

Now, does that make me *broken? Biased?*
Or just a product of my wiring and my *environment?*

Maybe it's the imprint—my dad made the switch not
long after I was born.
Maybe it's rebellion—people said I'd follow in his
footsteps,
so I tiptoed as far away from them as I could,
just to prove a point.
Or maybe, simplest of all: *I've always been drawn to
"other."*

I have soft curves. I want hard edges.
I have brown eyes. I want to drown in *green*,
get blinded by *hazel*,
or lose my sense of direction in *storm gray*.
I have brown hair—I crave *golds* and *reds* that catch
fire in the sun,

or *soft black that shines like oil under moonlight.*
I speak English.
So I want to *be asked "why?" and "what's wrong?"* or
told *"I like you"*
in a language that flows like poetry.

It's not about hating where I come from.
Black is beautiful—phenomenally so.
We don't crack. We age like myth.
But let's not pretend the cracks in *ivory and beige
and amber*
aren't just as breathtaking.
Different canvas. Still art.

Height? That's my only shallow hill to die on.
I'm 5'6". Not bad. Not tall. *But taller than him?*
No thanks.
Sorry. SUE ME.

So no, I'm not confused. I'm not ashamed.
I'm just **honest** about the weird, wonderful,
contradictory way
desire works when no one's policing it.

Turns out, preference isn't always political.
Sometimes it's just what makes your breath hitch.

Of Course I'd Marry Me

They used to ask me,
sometimes with curiosity, sometimes with warning
—

"Would you ever marry someone like you?"

And I'd answer without hesitation:
Yes.
Of course.
Why not?

But they'd look at me like I was missing something.
Like I hadn't yet figured out the *secret ugliness* hiding
inside me.
Like I was supposed to say no.
Supposed to cringe at the idea of being mirrored
too closely.
And eventually, I stopped saying yes out loud.

They told me people don't want someone like them
—

that if they saw their true selves in another,
they'd hate it.
That marriage to a mirror would be misery.
And I never fully understood that.
Still don't.

Because **I would marry me.**
Gladly.

I would marry the way I **listen** to people
talk about the random things they love—
just so they can hear themselves out loud
and *feel important for a moment.*

I would marry the way I remember *odd little facts*,
store them for years, and bring them back
in the perfect moment to build a bridge
between strangers who never thought they'd meet.

I would marry the way I ask questions that
cut past noise
and reach whatever part of you forgot it had a voice.

I would marry someone who *holds space*
without flinching or fidgeting.
Someone who doesn't get offended
when I say I need air,
but *nods* and *lets the silence stretch*
without packing it with guilt.

I don't understand people who say
marriage is constant work.
What are they fighting about?
Do they like blue and hate their partner for loving
green?

If I married me, we wouldn't need to match.
We'd just need to **respect**—
respect what we love,
respect what we're not,
respect how we show up to the world
with hands open, not clenched.

We'd have the same values,
the same *softness under the strength*,
the same *curiosity about life*,
the same *reverence for peace*,
the same refusal to turn **connection into
competition.**

We'd know before the vows
whether we wanted children,
where we wanted to live,
and what "*enough*" looked like.

Not because we agreed on everything,
but because we *named it early.*
Because **honesty** was always the language we spoke.

So yes.
I would marry me.
Not because I'm perfect.
But because I've done the work
to *not be afraid of my own reflection.*

That's what most people can't say.
That's why they warned me.
They thought love meant *hiding,*
bending, performing.
They thought being truly seen would feel like
judgment.

But me?
I want to be seen.
Not praised. Not fixed. Just seen.

So yes,
I would marry me.
And finally,
I've stopped feeling *guilty* for saying it out loud.

Tier 1 — Romantic Hire listing

📌 **Position: Love of My Life** *(Tall Enough to Ruin Me Edition)*
Location: *Wherever you are, I will find you.*
Start Date: *Immediately upon mutual eye contact and confirmed chemistry.*

- - -

💼 **Job Summary**:
Seeking a man who makes me want to *cancel plans, write bad poetry*, and question my life choices in the best way possible. This is a **high-intensity, high-reward** position with overtime in **affection, spontaneity**, and **physical attraction**.

- - -

✅ **Key Responsibilities**:

Height Management: *Minimum requirement — tall enough that I have to tilt my head back during arguments.*

Physical Compatibility: Must pass the *"carry me effortlessly"* test **without turning purple**.

Neanderthal Dane Viking Lumberjack Aesthetic: Broad, unapologetic shoulders; button-down shirt with rolled-up sleeves; optional suspenders; forearms that look like they've been carved out of oak. **Hands** should be wildly attractive — capable of opening jars, chopping wood, and distracting me mid-sentence. *Absolutely no Steve Urkel energy permitted.*

Romantic Chaos: *Surprise me.* Not with bills or emotional instability — just with trips, gifts, or showing up at my door because you missed me.

Affection Provision: *Cuddles on demand.* Slow-dancing in the kitchen is encouraged.

Verbal Fireworks: Make me laugh, challenge me in conversation, and occasionally say things that make me rethink my entire worldview.

Chemistry Maintenance: Keep the spark alive long enough that people still ask if we're newly dating **years** later.

📚 Qualifications:
Emotional intelligence: *High* — able to read my moods without me spelling them out.

Confidence: Secure enough to lead, humble enough to listen.

Lifestyle: Stable, but *never boring*.

Purity standards: Willing to match mine without me having to play FBI investigator.

Forearm game: Must be so strong it could distract me in the middle of a crisis.

💰 Compensation & Benefits:
Unmatched romantic access.

Exclusive rights to my softest moods and my wildest ideas.

A lifetime supply of inside jokes and private smiles.

The kind of **loyalty** that makes people wonder if I'm in a cult.

Disclaimer:
This is not the safe choice. This is the **I'll grow old with you but still want to make out in the laundry room** choice. **Proceed only if you can handle full-spectrum love with occasional thunderstorms.**

Tier 2 — Husband Job Listing

aka Marriage as a Business Transaction

📌 **Position: Steady Life Partner** *(Non-Romantic Division)*
Location: My house *(and yours, if you can pay for both)*
Start Date: *ASAP or whenever my patience for doing everything alone runs out.*

– – –

💼 **Job Summary**:
Seeking a **reliable, semi-entertaining male** to share bills, occasional meals, and the *illusion of companionship.* This is **not a romantic role** — think *"live-in co-CEO of household operations"* rather than *"soulmate."* Applicant must be **steady, non-chaotic**, and able to survive in *low-spark conditions*.

– – –

📋 **Key Responsibilities**:
Financial Stability: Must pay your share of bills on time, *without me having to chase you like a debt collector.*

Mild Entertainment: Should be able to make me laugh once in a while — not *every day, just enough so I don't regret the contract.*

Physical Presence: Sit beside me on the couch *without breathing too loudly* or scrolling TikTok at full volume.

Emotional Maintenance: Provide basic comfort when I'm upset (*hand on shoulder, one sympathetic nod*, do not attempt deep talks unless trained).

Conflict Management: Avoid turning minor disagreements into two-hour debates. Accept that sometimes *"because I said so"* is the final answer.

Self-Care: Maintain basic hygiene — deodorant is **mandatory**, cologne is optional. No *"au naturel"* experiments unless approved.

- - -

Qualifications:

Height: Equal to or taller than me (*non-negotiable; allergies to shortness apply*).

Emotional maturity: High enough to avoid tantrums, *low enough to let me have my way sometimes.*

Romantic ambition: *Low.* This is a slow-burn *"respect and fondness"* role, not a fireworks position.

Flexibility: Able to survive in a household where Netflix queue control is **70/30 in my favor.**

💰 **Compensation & Benefits**:

Shared financial load.

Mutual life stability.

Occasional cooked meals (*frequency negotiable*).

Lifetime membership to *"someone cares enough to pick you up from the airport."*

Disclaimer:

This is a no-grand-romance contract. Love may grow over time, but it will be the **I'd sign your cast if you broke your arm** kind — not the **write you poetry at midnight** kind.

It's easy to choose a husband.
Harder to choose **yourself.**

They say some babies **devour their twin**
in the womb.
I think I did.
But she never really left.

She became the *second mind humming under my
skin*—
the voice I could never shut off,
the one who saw the same room twice,
who lived in the margins of every decision.

One mind shines, *searching for paths*,
lighting corners no one else notices.
The other reflects,
dragging truths out of shadows
even when no one asked for them.

Together they tear through me—
the lantern and the mirror,
the guide and the judge,
the warmth and the exposure.

As a teen I thought it was a curse.
Everyone else moved like single lines,
pencils drawing one neat answer.

But I...
I was **ink bleeding sideways**,
branches of consequence I could see
but never erase.
I wanted to be simple.
I wanted to decide without dissecting.
I wanted to breathe without both lungs
arguing over how air should taste.

But I can't.
I never could.
Because I didn't just live—
I **inherited the ghost I swallowed.**

So maybe that's why people flinch around me,
why they clutch their mouths like pearls
when I pass—
I'm not one presence.
I'm two.
I draw you in with light,
then split you open with truth.

It isn't cruelty.
It isn't kindness.
It's just me.
The child who consumed her twin
and kept her voice alive.

Wholeness doesn't arrive in answers—it arrives in the permission to be **unfinished.**

If you've made it to this page,
I already know something about you.

You stayed.
You wandered through these unruly thoughts
with me.
You held space for the jagged edges, the soft echoes,
the things that didn't resolve neatly.
And that means more to me than I can say.

I don't know who you **are**.
I may never *meet* you,
laugh with you,
cry with you,
hug you,
or *kiss* you.

But believe me when I say—
with every fiber of my being—
that *I love you.*

Not the love we're taught to romanticize.
Not the one that demands performance or
permission.
But the kind of love that simply recognizes you.
That says: I see the ache in you. I see the beauty.
I see the fight and the quiet and the many selves
you've had to be just to keep going.
And I still call it all human.
All worthy.

I wrote this book for you—
even if I didn't know your name.
Even if I never do.

And if you carry even one line from this book with
you into the world,
I hope it reminds you that you're not strange for
feeling deeply,
not wrong for needing softness,
not alone in the questions you haven't yet answered.

I'm so grateful you let me speak to you in this way.
And if this book found you at the right time,
just know:
you were never lost.

I Appreciate You

Serenite

About the Author

Serenite Hope is a writer, poet, and observer of the human heart whose work blends raw honesty with quiet transformation. She believes stories don't need to be loud to leave an echo, and that the smallest, most fleeting moments often reveal the deepest truths.

Her writing is rooted in lived experience—exploring pain, resilience, identity, and the unexpected beauty found in ordinary life. With a voice that is both lyrical and unflinching, she creates pieces that invite readers to pause, reflect, and see themselves more clearly. Whether through poetry, poetic essays, or intimate short stories, her work refuses easy answers, preferring instead to provoke thought, stir emotion, and leave space for readers to carry their own meaning away.

Serenite's books—*Whispers of Healing, The Human Series (Every Shade of Human, this too, is human, a little too human and still, somehow, human) and Unformatted and Unscripted*—move between vulnerability and wit, seriousness and play. Each one weaves together poems, essays, haibun, and haiku in a style that resists convention, embracing both the polished and the imperfect as equally human.

Her writing has been described as a mirror and a lantern: it reflects what readers may not have words for, while also offering light to walk by.

Beyond the page, Serenite is drawn to culture, language, and connection. She explores Chinese dramas, music, and traditions with the same curiosity she brings to her writing, finding bridges between worlds and perspectives. Through her brand, RISELiftingOthers, she expands her reach across books, social platforms, and creative projects, encouraging kindness, authenticity, and courage in the face of conformity.

At her core, Serenite writes for those who feel "different" yet deeply human—for anyone who has ever carried unspoken pain, who has longed for recognition more than attention, and who seeks to build strength without losing softness. Her work reminds us that healing is not about erasing wounds but about discovering beauty, humor, and wisdom in every shade of being.

Meet the Vox

Serenite | The Eccentric Vox
Tour-Guiding Author Bum™
Builder of meaning, not skyscrapers

I was supposed to be an architect.
Instead, I became a tour guide through landscapes and language—
a storyteller wandering the edges of thought,
giving voice to what often remains unspoken.

Through poetry, personal essays, and raw reflections,
I explore identity, creativity, and the full spectrum of human experience.
My words are honest, layered, and unapologetic—
a compass made of memory and metaphor.

I don't write for *prestige*. I write for **presence**.
To laugh **loud**.
To question **deep**.

To remind us that value isn't found in résumés or rankings—
it's found in connection.

So no, I didn't become an architect.
I became a *Tour-Guiding Author Bum* with a backpack full of metaphors,
and a heart that beats to the rhythm of every story we almost didn't tell.

This is The Eccentric Vox.
Come wander with me.

www.riseliftingothers.com
serenitehope.substack.com
@TheEccentricVox
Facebook, Instagram, YouTube, Threads